THE ILLUSTRATED WINE MAKING BOOK

THE ILLUSTRATED WINE MAKING BOOK

Ralph Auf der Heide

PHOTOGRAPHS BY

Henry Fechtman

GARDEN CITY, NEW YORK

Doubleday & Company, Inc.

1973

ISBN: 0-385-04096-2
Library of Congress Catalog Card Number 72–90968
Copyright © 1973 by Ralph Auf der Heide
All Rights Reserved
Printed in the United States of America
First Edition

TO LISL

Acknowledgments

My grateful appreciation is extended to those who have been helpful in preparing this book: Leon McFadden, Tom Wilhelm, and Tony Rose, who prepared the preliminary photographs; Dr. Stanley Hill and Dennis Cogan of Santa Barbara, who allowed the use of their well-equipped cellars; Stanley Goodrich and Darrell Bassett, who generously placed materials and equipment at my disposal; Pierre La Fond, of the Santa Barbara Winery, for permission to photograph his establishment; Dick Smith, of the Santa Barbara *News Press*, for his neighborly advice and encouragement; and of course Henry Fechtman, whose photographs are an important part of the book.

I am especially indebted to my wife, who not only endured my neglect of other work but helped to assemble recipes and correct the manuscript.

CONTENTS

Zinfandel; Easy Wine Cake; Cullis; "Boil a Flounder
in the French Fashion"; Roasted Ham; Fricassee
of Mushrooms; "A Nice Sauce for Most Sorts of
Fish"; "To Stew Oysters, Cockels, and Muscles";
Chocolate Wine; Carrots Auf der Heide.

ILLUSTRATIONS

Introduction

Deep in the fragrant, glowing heart of each glass of wine lies a thread of history leading back beyond recorded time to the beginnings of human activity. The prehistoric cave dweller who first hesitantly tasted the bubbling liquid that spontaneously fermented from crushed fruit, and found it good, is unknown. We can only assume he enjoyed the effects. His attempts to repeat his discovery make wine making one of the earliest domestic activities. Thus, until very recently, most of the wine produced throughout the world was made in the home.

Even today, when enormous winery complexes employing scores of oenologists produce carloads of wine, many of the world's finest wineries are not much larger than home wine making projects. Romanée-Conti, producer of one of the supreme wines, has only four and a half acres of grapes, while its neighbor, La Romanée, has only two acres. From this tiny plot there is an annual production of a little more than twice as much as the home wine maker in the United States is allowed to make. Among the larger vineyards, the famous Clos de Vougeot, with 125 acres, is divided among more than fifty owners. Of these, only seventeen own more than one acre, while the largest proprietor owns fifteen acres. Many of the finest Rhine vineyards are tiny, and shared among several owners. For example, Rauenthaler Wülfen has seven acres.

The state owns 5.36 of these, while the remainder is split up among eight proprietors.

Wines from these vineyards enjoy world-wide reputations and sell for devastating prices. They are made with methods and equipment similar to those used by amateur wine makers. Stainless-steel stemmer/crushers, multiple-plate filters, and ion-exchange columns are all but unknown in these wineries, and are not necessary for the making of the finest homemade wines.

This book will provide basic information needed to make sturdy, honest wines. Add a little skill, more patience, and a certain amount of luck, and it will be possible to produce superb homemade wines.

The book is divided into sections that follow the natural sequence of preparing, making, and storing wine. Additional information is provided to make the use of wine most enjoyable, and to help keep your wine making efforts legal.

May the wines you make bring you much joy and rich rewards.

1

Making Wine – General Observations

Commercial wine making efforts are usually limited to wine made from grapes, although a few adventurous producers have included a limited number of fruit wines in their lists. Legal restrictions, designed to protect the public from adulterated products, prevent using some materials, while the high cost of making wine from rose hips, violets, orange blossoms, and similar ingredients, together with the possibility of their rejection by the buying public, effectively discourages experimentation.

Home wine makers have the advantage of using a large variety of materials from which to make wine, limited only by substances that are poisonous or disagreeable to taste. They can afford to spend the time and invest in the labor necessary to gather non-conventional wine ingredients and process them. The reward is a spectrum of exciting new taste experiences not to be found elsewhere in the realm of food and drink. Materials from which homemade wines can be made are conveniently divided into the following categories:

Fresh and dried fruits and berries
Flowers
Vegetables
Tubers

Herbs and spices
Cereals
Honey, concentrates, preserves, and miscellaneous.

The plan of this book is to allow the user to follow each step of the wine making process with as little need as possible to search in other parts of the book for information. Many of the operations for different kinds of wine are the same for all wines, so some repetition is inevitable. General observations on making wine follow:

The first step in making wine is to select the material from which it is to be made. Grapes, fruits, and berries should be tree- or vine-ripened, at the peak of their ripeness without being overripe, freshly picked, and free from mold, cuts, or

Wine grapes ready for processing. The whitish coating, or "bloom," on the skins consists primarily of thousands of yeast cells. (Photograph by Dick Smith)

bruises. Fruit with broken skins should be removed and discarded to avoid infecting the must with vinegar or other bacteria. These recommendations should not be interpreted to mean that the fruit should be perfect and absolutely free from blemishes. Surface imperfections, malformation, and bird damage that has healed are of no importance if they do not include breaks in the skin.

Flower wines should be made from blossoms only, without any stems, sepals, or other green parts. These are usually bitter and transmit this bitterness to the wine. Flowers should be picked in full blossom late in the morning of a sunny day so they are quite free from dew.

Tubers such as potatoes, carrots, etc. very often are more flavorful for wine making purposes when they are old than when freshly picked. This phenomenon is similar to the "sweating" that apples undergo before they are made into cider. Tubers may be best when they are old but should not be used if they are bruised, diseased, or moldy.

Herbs, like flowers, should be gathered after the sun has dried any dew. Herbs are best harvested when oils in the leaves are at the point of their maximum fragrance, which is generally reached just as the flowers open. Roots should be well cleaned and dried before use.

Spontaneous fermentation will occur when any fruit is crushed and natural yeasts are afforded a favorable environment in which to grow and reproduce and, incidentally, change sugar into alcohol and carbon dioxide. Wine makers take advantage of this natural process, guiding and controlling it to produce the type of wine desired. Since natural yeasts occurring on fruits and berries are of many different types and give different end results, it is best to eliminate them and work with pure strains of cultured wine yeasts. Natural, or wild, yeasts can be destroyed by pouring boiling water over the wine material, dosing it with sulfur dioxide, or both. While boiling water is usually sufficient to kill most of the wild yeasts, addition of sulfur dioxide in the form of potassium metabisulfite not only adds the *coup de grâce* but prevents musts from turning brown when exposed to air.

Small quantities of fruit and berries are easily crushed by hand. Squeezing ripe fruit into a vat is messy but not unpleasant. Larger quantities of fruit or berries may be crushed by being pounded with a pick handle or a pestle improvised from a piece of timber.

Any fruit, flowers, or herbs suspected of having spray residue or that are covered with dust should be washed in two waters. Uncontaminated wine making materials need only have boiling water poured over them. Firm-fleshed fruit such as apples and pears should be ground or chopped before fermenting. Grape crushers can be used for soft fruit and berries, as well as stone fruit that have had the pits removed.

Wine making recipes often specify an exact amount of sugar that is to be added to the fruit. There is nothing basically incorrect in this procedure, but the resulting wine can vary greatly in flavor, sweetness, and alcohol content, depending upon the amount of natural sugar contained in the fruit. More accurate controls over results are obtained if the given amount of boiling water is poured over the crushed fruit and allowed to cool to 70° F and a hydrometer reading is made of the juice and water to learn the amount of sugar needed to produce the kind of wine desired. In general, the amounts of fruit, sugar, and water should be calculated as shown below:

1. The fruit should be weighed.
2. Depending upon the type of wine desired, water should be added to make the following amounts:
    a. light table wines: 2½–3 pounds of fruit per gallon;
    b. medium wines: 3–5 pounds of fruit per gallon;
    c. robust, dessert wines: 4–6 pounds per gallon.
3. Sugar may then be added to obtain the following Balling readings on the hydrometer:
    a. light, dry table wines: 20–24°;
    b. medium wines: 26–32°;
    c. robust, sweet wines: 34–40°.

To obtain an increase of 1° Balling, ⅛ pound of sugar should be added to each gallon of must.

The most satisfactory way to incorporate sugar with the must is to extract approximately 1 pint of must for each pound of sugar to be dissolved. This liquid should be heated enough, and sugar stirred in until completely dissolved and clear; then the syrup is poured over the fruit and remaining must. Making a syrup has an advantage over simply adding sugar to the vat, because it mixes more rapidly and completely and changes to simple sugars more quickly than granulated sugar, which tends to sink to the bottom and take its own sweet time to dissolve. Granulated sugar, either cane or beet, is pure enough so that the syrup need not be boiled.

At this point the wine maker may wish to check the acidity of the must and, if necessary, correct it. (See page 56)

As with any other plant, yeasts thrive when enough nutrients are available to them. Grapes, berries, and most fruit are blessed with sufficient nutrients to establish and maintain vigorous yeast activity. Addition of nutrients in the form of raisins or ammonia salts is indicated for flower, herb, tuber, and most other wines lacking in adequate nutrient materials.

Tannin is necessary for proper maturing of red and white grape wines and gives better balance to fruit and berry wines as well. Most red grape wines and those made from elderberries, pears, and chokecherries have sufficient natural tannin. Added to other wine materials, tannin will be beneficial and improve quality.

Fruit, berry, and white wines made from grapes benefit from addition of pectic enzymes to freshly crushed must. They break down natural pectins contained in the fruit, which often cause hazy wines that can never satisfactorily be cleared by home methods. Enzymes also inhibit the jelling effect of fruit pectins, thus releasing more juice. For these reasons pectic enzymes are recommended in fruit-wine and berry-wine production.

When the must has been corrected as described above, sterilized, and cooled to room temperature, pure wine-yeast cultures may be added, and active fermentation will commence. Dry yeast may be added directly from the package, while agar slants or liquid yeasts must be "started" about three days before being used, so that a large colony of active cells are present for vigorous fermentation.

After yeast has been added, the fermenting vat should be covered and allowed to stand from eight to twenty-four hours. If plastic vats with covers are used, no other precautions are needed. Metal covers can be used if a tightly woven clean cloth is placed over the top of the fermentation vat and the metal cover put on top of the cloth. The cloth catches any drops of condensed moisture that may carry tiny amounts of dissolved metal, which might contaminate the wine.

In spite of the need for yeasts to have oxygen for their healthy growth, once vigorous fermentation has started the vat should be closed with a tight cover. Enzymes can still do their job of sugar conversion, but yeasts are prevented from oxidizing part of the alcohol into unpleasant-tasting end products. Enough air for continuing healthy fermentation will be supplied by daily stirring of the must and punching down the cap. The cap, or chapeau, consists of light pulp and other particles carried to the surface by bubbles of carbon dioxide and held there because they are not heavy enough to sink. If the cap were allowed to remain without being stirred down into the liquid, acetic bacteria would have plenty of air and freedom to multiply and turn the wine to vinegar. When the must is stirred, any small Acetobacter colonies are submerged without a source of available oxygen and cannot survive.

After the must is stirred, temperature and hydrometer readings are taken and recorded in the wine logbook. Records kept in this manner are a guide to future wine making efforts and may provide valuable clues for ways to improve cellar operations.

Crushed grapes—fresh must before fermentation is started.
(Photograph by Dick Smith)

Wine temperatures rise when energy is released by conversion of sugar into alcohol and carbon dioxide, and stirring equalizes temperatures in the various layers of the liquid, allowing accurate thermometer readings to be made. A slight rise in temperature can be tolerated, but if the thermometer goes above 75° F, there may be trouble ahead and prompt steps to reduce temperature are advised. The must can be cooled by holding a plastic bucket or a glass jug filled with cold or ice water in the fermenting vat until the temperature falls to acceptable limits. In cold climates an abrupt drop in temperature may inhibit yeast activity and lead to stuck fermentation unless a jug of hot water is used to warm the must. After the must temperature has risen, vigorous stirring often helps to restore yeast activity. In some cases, however, it will be necessary to reinoculate the must with a fresh yeast culture. In any case, close observation of temperature and hydrometer readings will help the wine maker to anticipate problems before they become too critical.

Many wine making recipes not only specify exact amounts of sugar to be added to the fruit, no matter how full of natural sugar, but state without equivocation that active fermentation should last an exactly specified length of time and then be terminated. The times given in various recipes vary widely. Such arbitrary time limits, without regard to ambient temperatures, yeast virility, or other conditions affecting the course of fermentation, may result in a good wine, but may just as easily end in disaster. The only valid way to determine when active fermentation should be halted, and secondary fermentation commenced, is to be guided by the hydrometer.

For white grape wine and other musts that have been pressed before fermentation, where a minimum of solid pulp is present, the wine is allowed to reach a hydrometer reading of zero Balling before being transferred to a closed, secondary fermenter. For red grape wines and all other wines in which pressing follows fermentation, primary fermentation is terminated when the hydrometer reads between 4° and 6° Balling. The reason for treating musts *to be pressed* differently from those *pressed before fermenting* is that pressing results in a violent environmental change for the yeasts, which are to continue fermentation processes during secondary fermentation. They are thought to recover from the shock better if a fairly large amount of sugar still remains for them to feed upon. Wines pressed prior to fermentation, and simply transferred from an open to a closed container for secondary fermentation, do not undergo drastic changes and do not require the added cushion of sugar.

In secondary fermentation, only young wine separated from pulp or pomace is used. Wine and pomace may be separated in several different ways: for example, pulp may be dipped out of the fermenting vat with a plastic colander or strainer and placed in a pressing bag; or a plastic tube with plastic netting over the end submerged in the wine can be placed in the vat, with the liquid siphoned and strained out at the same time. In any case, as much free-run juice as possible should be strained from the pomace.

The pomace, or pulp remaining after juice has drained off, is treated in different ways, depending upon the type of wine

Secondary fermentation in 5-gallon jug, showing water seal.

desired. The finest red grape wines are often made with only free-run juice, with pressed juice becoming a secondary wine. In many cases pomace is gently pressed one time, and the juice from that pressing is added to the free-run juice. Second and third pressings are often made in commercial wineries, but these are usually kept separate from the free-run and first-press juices. Juice from second and third pressings is usually harsher, contains more solids, and requires longer to mature. Another technique used by amateur wine makers to stretch their supply of grapes is to make a secondary wine from the pomace after the free-run juice has drained off. This is done by replacing the free-run juice with the same amount of water, adding sugar to equal the original Balling reading, and refermenting.

Secondary fermentation is generally slower and less violent than primary. It should take place with an absolute minimum of contact with air. If glass jugs or carboys are used, they should be filled to within one to one and a half inches of the brim. If barrels are employed, they should be filled as full as possible without running over. In order to exclude air, yet allow carbon dioxide to escape and not blow up the container, some sort of relief valve must be provided. Traditionally, this has consisted of many different devices, all the way from grape leaves placed over the bunghole of a barrel and held down by a bag of sand, to heavy, brown paper pasted over the bunghole. "Water seals" or "fermentation locks" are customarily recommended for this purpose. These consist of a tube that passes from the wine container through a cork into a glass full of water. Carbon dioxide generated by fermenting wine flows through the tube into the water, where it bubbles out into the atmosphere. The water in the glass prevents air from entering the container through the tube but does not restrict the exit of carbon dioxide. While these devices are quite efficient as long as water covers the end of the tube, evaporation can destroy their effectiveness.

A much simpler method for preventing air from reaching

Secondary fermentation in gallon jugs, showing Saran Wrap seal.

Polyethylene containers for secondary fermentation and temporary storage of wine. From the left: rigid 5-gallon container, collapsible 5-gallon, 2½-gallon, and 1-gallon containers.

First racking. The end of the tube from which the wine flows is placed high in the neck, so the wine spreads over the inside surface of the glass and is aerated.

wine, and yet allowing the release of internal pressure, is to use a thin piece of Saran Wrap held in place by rubber bands. The rubber bands stretch, allowing carbon dioxide to escape, then return to their original tightness to prevent air from entering the wine container. The film is impervious to air and will not crack or become brittle during the time it protects the wine, costs less, and is more reliable than fermentation locks. Such membranes of plastic film have protected bottles of my wine for at least four years with no loss of integrity. To place them on bottles or jugs, simply lay the

Second (and subsequent) racking. The tube outlet is placed at the bottom of the receiving jug to reduce the wine surface exposed to air.

film over the neck of the bottle and stretch a rubber band over it and the neck of the bottle to hold it down. For barrels, the same effect can be achieved by drilling a hole in a bung, driving it tightly into the bunghole, placing the plastic over the top of the bung, and holding it down with a rubber band in the same manner as with the glass jug. With this protection there is never any worry that the water has evaporated from the water seal and left the wine vulnerable to exposure to air. However, wine will evaporate through barrel staves and must be replaced with new wine.

After about thirty days, or when a noticeable layer of sediment is deposited on the bottom of the glass jug, the new wine should be siphoned or "racked" off into a fresh container, leaving the deposit behind. For this first racking, the outlet of the tube should be near the top of the receiving container so the wine can be slightly aerated as it flows down the inside surface of the jug. This small amount of added air helps the wine to mature. After racking, the water seal or new plastic film is replaced and the wine allowed to remain quiet for about ninety days more, when the second racking should take place. The second and subsequent rackings should be made with the outlet of the siphon tube at the bottom of the container so only the top surface of the wine is exposed to air and minimum aeration takes place. This reduces the chances of acetic acid development.

The wine maker now discovers why many containers of different sizes are necessary. If secondary fermentation began with a 5-gallon jug full of wine, and racking left a layer of lees amounting to a quart of residue, then a quart of new wine of the same type must be added to fill the container. If no wine of the same type is available, then pure water must be added to "top off" the container, or the contents must be transferred to some smaller bottles—for example, four 1-gallon jugs, one ½-gallon jug, and one or more fifths. Each of these containers must immediately be labeled so that one knows what is being tasted when the wine is finally ready. When barrels are used, evaporation losses must be added to racking losses, because wine evaporating through pores in the wood must be replaced on a weekly basis if air in the barrel is to be kept to a minimum. Losses from evaporation in barrels can become extremely discouraging if a small amount of wine is aged in that type of container.

When the wine is completely clear, and all fermentation has stopped, it is ready to bottle.

In order to bottle wine so that it can remain potable until it has reached maturity, the following items are needed:

—wine that has completed fermentation
—clean bottles
—sterile corks
—six feet of sterile surgical tubing
—a bottle corker
—a mallet.

Bottle-washing machine. Water is pumped from the container up to the bottom of the bottle, while brushes clean the inside. Waste water flows out through the tubing and does not mix with the clean water.

Clean bottles are an absolute requirement to properly age and store wines. Used bottles should be washed in a solution of sal soda and water, then thoroughly rinsed. Brushes with long crank-type handles are convenient for removing ordinary dirt. A 16-inch length of galvanized chain, small enough in diameter to fit inside the neck of a wine bottle, tied to a length of nylon cord that is in turn fastened to a cork, is useful for removing stubborn deposits. The full length of the chain is dropped into a bottle partly filled with water. One hand is placed over the neck to keep water and chain from falling out; then the bottle is rotated and shaken to swirl the chain around the inside. This will dislodge all but the most stubborn dirt. This device is easier to use and more

Chain attached to cork for cleaning bottles.

Cleaning bottles by swirling chain in solution of washing soda.

efficient than the handful of gravel sometimes recommended. The nylon cord allows the hand to hold the water in and allows easy removal of the chain without its bunching up in the neck, while the cork attached to the end of the cord makes the chain easy to locate even in sudsy water. If dirt still remains in the bottle after scouring it with the chain, throw the bottle away; it will never get clean.

A length of aluminum tubing bent to a U shape and attached to a faucet fitting is an excellent device for rinsing bottles. After bottles are cleaned and drained, a recommended finishing touch is to place a funnel in the neck and fill the bottle with a solution of potassium metabisulfite. The funnel is then placed in the next bottle and the solution poured from the first into the second bottle, making sure that the neck of the bottle from which liquid is poured is dipped into the potassium metabisulfite solution that fills the

Sterilizing bottles by pouring potassium metabisulfite solution from one cleaned bottle to another. Note the neck of bottle dipped into the liquid in the funnel.

funnel. This process is repeated until all the cleaned, rinsed bottles have been filled with the potassium metabisulfite solution. The few drops of solution remaining in the bottom of each bottle should not be drained out, but should be left in while the bottle is being filled with wine. This will provide an additional few parts per million of sulfur dioxide to help preserve the wine. By using a fairly high concentration of potassium metabisulfite, i.e. 10 grams per ⅕ gallon, no potassium metabisulfite other than that left after the sterilization should be necessary.

Corks are best sterilized and softened at the same time by steaming over boiling water in a closed container for twenty minutes. A vegetable steamer is excellent for this purpose, keeping the corks from being soaked in the water but killing all microorganisms in the cracks. After sterilization, corks should be handled carefully so they will not contaminate the bottled wine. If corks are simply boiled, they absorb so much water that air pressure generated when they are driven into the neck of the bottle is often enough to force the corks part-way back out.

Siphoning is the best way to move wine from storage containers to bottles. A very useful siphon can be made by attaching a 6-foot length of surgical tubing to a 3-foot length of plexiglass tube of the same inside diameter. Before attaching the rubber to the plexiglass, about four inches of that end of the tube should be softened in a flame. After the plexiglass is softened, it should be bent to curve like a walking stick. This will prevent the rubber from pinching as the siphon curves over the container. The other end of the plexiglass tube should be cut to a sharp angle, so the end can stand in the sediment at the bottom of the container while the opening through which the wine flows is above that layer. Using small-diameter, flexible siphon tubing allows the bottle to be filled from the bottom with minimum absorption of air, as well as permitting accurate control over the flow by pinching the tube with the fingers. Filling bottles by pouring

Filling bottles by siphoning wine from secondary-fermentation jugs.

from a spigot is not recommended, because it tends to excessively aerate the wine.

For small quantities of wine, the simplest corkers are quite adequate. If the corker is lubricated from time to time with PAM, a vegetable spray-on coating used to keep food from sticking to pans during cooking, it will be easy to seat corks from ⅞ to ¹⁵⁄₁₆ inch in diameter.

Temporary labels, for use while wine is being stored, are best made from smooth white masking tape. These adhere well to bottles and yet can be removed when the bottle is reused. White tape provides a better background for the writing than does the cream-colored tape. Information should be written with a fine-pointed felt pen containing waterproof

ink. Water-soluble ink will rub off and disappear long before
the wine is ready to be used. The label should be applied
upside down, to the shoulder of the bottle. This will allow
ready identification of bottles stored on their sides if the
corks face outward.

*Preparing to cork a bottle. The cork has been inserted in the
opening of the corker, and the plunger rests on top of the cork.*

Suitable permanent labels can be designed by the individual or reproduced from old engravings or woodcuts. The attached label originated as half of an engraving illustrating an old German edition of *Faust*. The other part of the picture was removed during the processing by a photoengraver, leaving the vine-leaf/cellar-door motif.

Labels improvised from old prints and engravings.

2

Licenses, Equipment, and Chemicals

Each head of a family in the United States is allowed by federal regulation to make up to two hundred gallons of wine yearly for his family use without payment of tax. If state laws prohibit wine making, they take precedence over federal regulations. There has recently been an attempt in Congress to change the regulations so as to allow single persons not the heads of households to make up to one hundred gallons of wine annually, but, as of the time of this writing, these changes have not taken effect. In order to legally make wine at home, the head of a household must send for Form 1541, which is shown, fill out two copies, and send them to the local Assistant Regional Commissioner, Alcohol, Tobacco, and Firearms Division, Internal Revenue Service. A list of district offices is included in the Appendix. When the Assistant Regional Commissioner receives the forms, which should be sent to him at least five days before wine making is started, he stamps and initials one copy and returns it to be kept available for inspection. No fee or charge is made in connection with the permit. The reverse of the form contains the pertinent regulations, which are quite easy and simple to understand, and when followed, eliminate any question about the individual's right to make his allocation of wine.

Important to peace of mind, and vital to family acceptance

FORM 1541
(REV. JULY 1970)

DEPARTMENT OF THE TREASURY - INTERNAL REVENUE SERVICE
REGISTRATION FOR PRODUCTION OF WINE FOR FAMILY USE
(See Instructions on back)

TO: Assistant Regional Commissioner (Alcohol, Tobacco and Firearms) *(City and State)*

P. O. Box 1991 Main Office, Los Angeles, Calif. 90053

FROM: *(Print or type your name and address below)*

PLEASE RETURN BOTH COPIES

ASSISTANT REGIONAL
COMMISSIONER'S STAMP

(Date Received)

NAME
AND
ADDRESS

*(Number,
Street,
City,
State,
ZIP Code)*

PART I — NOTICE OF REGISTRATION

1. I intend to begin production of not more than 200 gallons of wine annually, solely for my family use, on or about the date indicated at right.

DATE

2. The wine will be produced and stored at (Number, Street, City, State, ZIP Code. If rural address, show county, name or number of highway, and approximate distance and direction from registrant's post office.)

	Check (√)		6. I understand that the filing of this notice—
	Yes	No	
3. Are you the head of a family?.....................................			(a) does not give me authority to sell the wine produced;
4. Are you single?...			
If so, do any dependents live with you?..........................			(b) does not give me authority to make wine in partnership with another person;
5. Are you married?...			
If so, do wife (husband) or other dependents live with you?..			(c) does not give me authority to make wine for a person not a member of my family.

7. I also understand that if I sell any of the wine or otherwise do not comply with the law, and with the regulations stated on the back of this form, I will be subject to the penalties imposed by internal revenue law.

8. Under penalties of perjury, I declare that I have examined this Notice of Registration and to the best of my knowledge and belief, it is true, correct, and complete.

DATE

SIGNATURE

PART II — WINE PRODUCED

Date (a)	Kind (Grape, blackberry, cherry, etc.) (b)	Gallons (c)

FORM 1541 (REV. 7-70)

INSTRUCTIONS

1. General. Internal revenue law and regulations provide that the head of any family may, without payment of tax, produce not more than 200 gallons of wine a year for the use of his family, and not for sale, if he registers to do so. Under these provisions, a person is considered to be the head of a family only if he exercises family control or responsibility over one or more individuals closely connected with him by blood relationship or relationship by marriage, or by adoption, and who are living with him in one household. Anyone who intends to produce more than 200 gallons of wine a year, or who intends to produce any wine for sale, cannot cover such production by means of this registration, but must obtain a permit from the Assistant Regional Commissioner (Alcohol, Tobacco and Firearms), file bond and meet other requirements for the operation of a bonded wine cellar.

2. Registration. The head of a family who intends to produce wine for family use must complete this form in duplicate and send both copies to the Assistant Regional Commissioner (Alcohol, Tobacco and Firearms) at least 5 days before he begins to produce the wine. The Assistant Regional Commissioner will keep one copy and return the other to the registrant. When wine is produced, the registrant must record on this form, in Part II, the date of production, the kind of wine, and the gallons produced. The producer should keep his copy of the form available for inspection and examination by Government officers.

IT IS UNLAWFUL TO PRODUCE WINE FOR FAMILY USE WITHOUT FILING THIS NOTICE.

PERTINENT REGULATIONS

Part 240 (Wine), title 26, of the Code of Federal Regulations contains the following provisions relative to the production of wine for family use:

Section 240.540 *Registered producer.*—A duly registered head of any family may produce annually for family use, and not for sale, not in excess of 200 gallons of wine without payment of tax. A person is deemed to be the head of a family only if he exercises family control or responsibility over one or more individuals closely connected with him by blood relationship, relationship by marriage, or by adoption, and who are living with him in one household. This exemption does not authorize the production of wine for such use contrary to State law.

Section 240.541 *Limitations of exemption.*—The statutory exemption does not apply to (a) wine made by one person for use of another, whether consumed on the premises or removed therefrom for the family use of the owner; (b) wine produced by a single person unless he is the head of a family; (c) wine produced by a married man living apart from his family; (d) wine made by a partnership, except as provided in §240.730, or produced at a bonded wine cellar by two or more heads of families jointly; (e) wine produced by a corporation or association; or (f) wine furnished to persons not members of the producer's family.

Section 240.542 *Registration, Form 1541.*—Every person (other than the operator of a bonded wine cellar) coming within the statutory exemption and desiring to produce wine for the exclusive use of his family shall file Form 1541, in accordance with the instructions on the form. Upon production of the wine, the registrant will enter the quantity produced and the date of production on the copy of the form returned to him by the assistant regional commissioner. Such form shall be retained at the place of production while the wine produced pursuant thereto remains on hand. A new form shall be submitted each succeeding year during which it is desired to produce wine for family use, the year to be reckoned as commencing on July 1 and ending on June 30 following.

Section 240.543 *Removal of wine.*—Wine made for family use may not be removed from the premises where made without authority of the assistant regional commissioner.

Section 240.730 *Removal for family use.*—Where the head of a family as defined in §240.541, operates a bonded wine cellar as an individual owner, or in partnership solely with members of such family, wine of his own production not exceeding 200 gallons per year, may be removed without payment of tax for use of his family, the year to be reckoned as commencing July 1. The proprietor must make entries of quantities so removed in his monthly report, Form 702. Wine in excess of the 200 gallon allowance removed from the wine cellar for family use must be reported as a taxable removal.

Internal Revenue Service Form 1541. Front and reverse.

Polyethylene wastebaskets of various sizes, used as primary-fermentation vats.

of wine making activities, is the location of the winery. Ideally, part of a basement should be set aside for these activities. In addition to a cool, quiet area for long-term wine storage, it should have a good-sized sink, a stove or a hot plate for boiling water or other ingredients, and a place for storage of equipment. A concrete floor with adequate drainage makes sanitation easy. Most present-day houses are built without basements, so an alternative solution is to set aside part of a garage, service porch, or kitchen. If wine is to be made in the kitchen, a nearby inside closet should be requisitioned so that fermenting wines need not be disturbed. Equipment and utensils can be stored in a box, except for crushers and presses, which take up too much room. In planning a winery it is best to look for a location that will be out of the way, easily cleaned, and will not interfere with daily functioning of the household.

A fundamental piece of wine making equipment is the vat used for open, or primary, fermentation. Traditionally this has been an oak barrel or a redwood tub, an enamel pot, or a ceramic crock. In the past few years, inexpensive, lightweight, impermeable, easily cleaned polyethylene containers have become available, and except for dyed-in-the-wool traditionalists, have been almost universally accepted. These containers come in various forms, from heavy-duty industrial tanks having capacities from five hundred to a thousand gallons, to wastebaskets holding only a few quarts. It is best to buy vats large enough to contain the largest amount of fermentation material to be used, and of the heaviest construction available. The proper size for a primary fermentation vat is approximately one fourth larger than the greatest amount of must to be fermented. Foam and froth are generated during initial fermentation but can be contained without spilling if the vat is large enough.

Various types of wine making equipment. From left to right: stainless-steel bucket, hand crusher, stirring paddle, funnels, barrel, corks and a bung loosener, bottle, and another crusher.

In planning how much wine to make, it is well to remember that the largest investment in the entire process will be in *time*. Time required to clear and age the wine. While it is certainly possible to make another batch when the first runs out, another year or two may pass before the new wine develops its best flavor. Wine also has a sneaky way of disappearing just as it reaches its peak of mature quality. First, there is the necessary tasting to determine if the wine is developing properly, then the family is asked to make a judgment, and later, the greatest drain of all, the finished product is shared with friends and admirers. Taking these inevitable withdrawals into consideration, five gallons appears to be the absolute minimum amount to make of any wine. For purely experimental wines, one-gallon lots may be made, but this quantity is inadequate for any real aging or large-scale enjoyment.

If possible, fermenting vats should be bought with covers. While a certain amount of oxygen is necessary for yeasts to grow and multiply, this is supplied during the daily stirring of the must. The rest of the time, air should be excluded by a close-fitting cover. Another recommended precaution is to select containers with the fewest corners and crevices. Industrial designers and mold makers feel they must justify themselves by impressing a design or pattern on the product. In fermenting vats these embellishments simply make cleaning more difficult and should be avoided if possible. Plastic containers other than polyethylene should not be used. They are made with volatile plasticizers, which can evaporate into the wine, adding a nasty taste.

The most satisfactory way to transfer wine from one container to another is by siphoning, or "racking" as it is called by wine makers. Any attempt to pour wine, no matter how carefully done, stirs up sediment from the bottom of the container and allows air to get into the wine. Both these undesirable conditions are minimized by proper siphoning equipment. Thin-walled, transparent plastic tubing or surgical rubber are both satisfactory materials for siphon tubing. The flexible tube is best attached to a rigid plexiglass tube of similar diameter that has had one end heated and curved like the handle of a cane. The other end should be cut at a sharp angle so the tip can rest on the bottom of the container while siphoning action takes place about three-quarters inch from the bottom, thus avoiding inclusion of sediment with the liquid being siphoned. It is best to avoid tubing with heavy walls, since this makes quick stopping of the flow difficult— very important when bottles are being filled and overflow is imminent. The most satisfactory diameter for home wine making ranges from one-quarter to five-eighths inch internal diameter. Smaller tubing transfers fluids too slowly, while anything larger creates a serious vortex, which can stir up too much sediment. Siphoning should be started and terminated gradually, pinching the tubing to restrict flow. A rapid surge of pressure can withdraw excessive amounts of sediment. It is also a good idea to start the siphoning process with the withdrawing end of the tube close to the surface of the fluid being withdrawn, gradually lowering the end of the tube until its opening is just above the surface of the deposit. When the last two or three inches of liquid is all that remains, the tube should once again be pinched closer, to reduce the amount of unwanted sediment. Containers being racked can be tilted to increase the amount of clear liquid that can be removed.

Plastic funnels of various sizes are useful in "topping off" or other operations in which sugar, thin pulp, or liquids are to go into narrow-necked bottles. A small funnel is indispensable for decanting wine from its storage bottle into a serving decanter.

Thin plastic sheeting, such as that used to protect food, is a convenient material to use during secondary fermentation and aging. Stretched over the neck of a bottle, and held on with a rubber band, it provides an effective and reliable seal to keep air from reaching the wine, and yet permits accumulating carbon dioxide generated by fermentation to escape

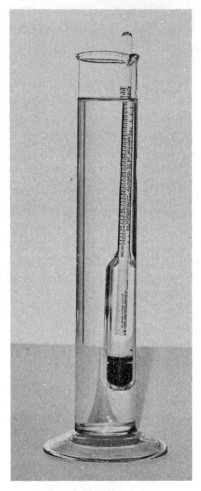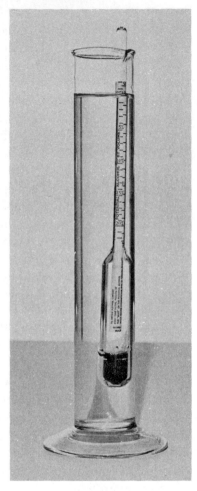

Hydrometers, showing potential-alcohol and Balling scales.

without building up dangerous pressures. Plastic film is an inexpensive, dependable substitute for fermentation locks, which have an annoying habit of running dry and leaving the wine unprotected.

Heavier plastic, such as sheet polyethylene, available in thicknesses of from two to ten mils, and widths from three to twenty feet, can be used in many ways. Fermentation-vat covers, anti-splash protectors, gigantic funnels, and floor protectors are just a few of the uses for plastic sheeting.

The suitability of juice for fermentation, progress of fermentation, and the health of the developing wine are all measured by the hydrometer and the thermometer. Hydrometers, frequently called saccharometers, are weighted glass tubes with one or more scales printed on a piece of paper sealed inside. Scales usually shown are specific gravity; Balling (or Brix), which indicates the proportion of solids (sugar) in the liquid; and percentage of potential alcohol.

The specific gravity of distilled water at sea level, when the temperature is 60° F, is shown as 1.000. For wine making, the specific gravity scale should range from about .990 to about 1.170. This range will correspond to a Balling scale of −4° to +44.4°, and a potential-alcohol scale of −2% to +22.2%. The Balling and Brix scales, so named after the individuals who developed them, measure the sugar content of must, and since 2° on the Balling scale ferments out to 1 per cent alcohol, the two scales, Balling (Brix) and potential alcohol, are easily related.

The most accurate hydrometer measurements are made when the liquid to be measured is placed in a long narrow tube called the hydrometer jar. The jar should be filled about two-thirds full, so that adding the hydrometer will not make the liquid overflow. As the hydrometer is lowered into the liquid, it is swirled to brush off any bubbles that might adhere to it and raise the hydrometer higher in the fluid than an actual concentration of solids. It is then gently forced to the bottom of the jar and allowed to rise to its floating position. The point on the scale even with the liquid surface is read by placing the eye parallel to the top of the fluid. The small amount that curves up against the sides of the hydrometer should not be considered in the reading. Rough measurements

SPECIFIC GRAVITY	BALLING (°) (BRIX)	POTENTIAL ALCOHOL (%)	
.990	− 3.5	− 1.8	
1.000	0	0	
1.010	+ 2.6	+ 1.3	
1.020	5.4	2.7	
1.030	7.7	3.8	
1.040	10.1	5	
1.050	12	6	
1.060	15	7.5	
1.070	17.5	8.7	
1.080	19.7	9.8	
1.090	22	11	(dry wine)
1.100	24	12	
1.110	26.2	13	
1.120	28.2	14	(medium
1.130	30.2	15	wine)
1.140	32	16	
1.150	34.5	17.2	(sweet
1.160	36.2	18	wine)
1.170	38	19	

When wine reaches 1.000 on the specific gravity scale after fermenting, it is not completely dry, with all sugar changed to alcohol and carbon dioxide, but still retains approximately 1.5° Balling of unfermented sugar. This anomaly is explained by the fact that after fermentation at sp. gr. 1.000, about 11 per cent of the total volume is alcohol, which has a sp. gr. of only .7938. The lighter liquid counterbalances the heavier sugar remaining in solution, causing the discrepancy. The same sort of inaccuracy is met in testing fresh must. About 1.5° of the reading must be subtracted to compensate for solids in the fluid that are not sugar. After the must has stood several hours, these solids are deposited, and the hydrometer reading reflects the true sugar concentration.

of fermenting liquids can be made by floating the hydrometer directly in the vat, providing not too much pulp is contained in the top layer. Greatest accuracy is obtained by using strained liquid in a jar.

Most hydrometers are calibrated to read correctly at 60° F,

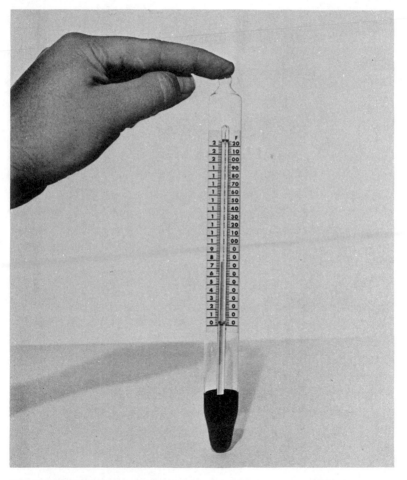

Floating-type thermometer, used for determining temperature of musts and wines.

Taking a hydrometer reading. The hydrometer has just been pushed into the must to remove any air bubbles and to be certain that the hydrometer floats freely. The eye should be level with the surface of the liquid. (Photograph by Leon McFadden)

so differences in temperature should be considered when readings are taken. Variations of .25° Balling at 50° F, and .84° Balling at 80° F are possible in a fluid containing 20° Balling of sugar. Amateur wine makers generally consider these as insignificant and safely ignored.

Hydrometers not only measure the original sugar content of the must, and thus can help determine when fruit is ripe, but can also chart the progress of fermentation. During active fermentation, musts should be thoroughly stirred at least once a day, the temperature read, and a hydrometer measurement made. These will show whether an active fermentation is taking place or if the fermentation has "stuck." The same hydrometer reading two or three days in a row indicates that fermentation has stopped and reactivation is necessary.

For musts that are to be pressed after fermentation, primary fermentation is stopped when the Balling reading reaches between 6° and 4°. Musts to be racked without pressing, or that were pressed before fermentation, can generally go to zero Balling. These differences are justified by the great change in conditions that takes place when pomace is removed from the must. Allowing more sugar to remain in the solution means that fermentation has a better chance of resuming when the pressing is completed and the wine removed to the secondary fermenter. For wines that need no pressing, but are simply racked from the fermentation vat to the enclosed secondary fermentation vessel, as is the case with white wine made from grapes, the transition is less of a shock, and chances of stuck fermentation are very small.

When wine is placed in a closed container, with most of the pulp removed, the container is completely filled and air is prevented from reaching the wine; then secondary fermentation begins. This distinction between primary and secondary fermentation is quite artificial as far as the yeasts are concerned. They continue to function as before, changing sugar to alcohol and CO_2 until all sugar is consumed, or until they are killed by the alcohol they have made. The step of removing the wine from the open vat and placing it in a sealed bottle simply reduces the chances of having the wine turn to vinegar, by allowing only minimal contact with air, which is necessary for the growth and development of the Acetobacter.

Healthy wine is cool wine. As mentioned before, thermometer readings should be made on a daily basis, particularly if the volume of liquid is large and the fermenting vat is made of a relatively poor thermal conductor such as wood. Home wine makers should not permit must temperatures to exceed 75° F, if at all possible. Lower temperatures will provide somewhat less alcohol in the finished product, but generally the wine will have better flavor. Undesirable yeast and bacterial activity take place much more readily at elevated temperatures, and yeast activity is drastically curtailed at 84° F. It is interesting to note, as reported in the *Journal of the American Society of Enology*, that the average temperature at which red wines are fermented in eight "superior" Napa Valley wineries ranges between 70° F and 80° F, while white-wine temperatures range between 45° F and 55° F. Commercial wineries, with their heat exchangers and refrigeration equipment, can maintain much closer control over fermentation temperatures. So in cases where flavor is improved by higher temperature fermentation, as with Pinot Noir grapes, they

Wine making equipment. In the foreground is a polyethylene colander, used as a dipper to remove pulp and skins from primary fermenter. To the side is a rack used between "cheeses" in rack presses. At the rear is a grid to be placed under a roller crusher to collect stems. The grapes drop between the threads, which are made of 40-pound-test monofilament fishline.

Pressing bag and small, nutcracker-type press. The bag containing skins and pulp is pressed between the two boards. Knots in the rope permit the spacing to be adjusted for bags containing different amounts of material.

can afford to skirt upper temperature boundaries. Home wine makers must sacrifice some possible improvement in final product for reliable results.

Long-handled, hardwood stirring paddles may be bought at most restaurant-supply houses, or an acceptable substitute can be made from a 3-foot length of 1×3-inch redwood. Before being used, it should be sterilized by boiling, and thereafter cleaned by rinsing immediately before and after each use, with precautionary boiling after each active fermentation is completed. The paddle should be kept in an airy location so it does not become moldy. It should also be protected against accumulating too much dust.

Amateur wine makers will generally require two types of strainers: One, with rather large openings, useful for dipping pulp out of primary-fermentation vats, is typically a polyethylene colander similar to the type shown in the accompanying picture. The other, with a much finer mesh, is useful for removing small particles, and, when necessary, as a support for filter paper. Both strainers should be large enough to handle sizable amounts of liquid or pulp and be made of stainless steel or food-approved plastic. Strainers of this sort are also available from restaurant-supply houses. An improvised strainer can be made from plastic window screening attached to a redwood frame. For strainers of this type, the screening should be held in place with wood strips, so the weight of the pulp will not tear it away from the edge.

Pressing bags are best made of a loosely woven material sewed with at least three rows of stitching at the seams. Cotton, nylon, and Dacron* are recommended materials. Woven Saran† cloth, used for shading plants, makes excellent pressing cloths. Window screening made of plastic can also be used. After the free-run juice has been removed, the remaining pomace is put into the pressing bag and squeezed to remove the liquid. Handling the pomace is easier and less messy when bags are used in conventional basket presses, and they are required for flat-bed, or hand, pressing. A pressing cloth, which is a flat sheet of the same type of open-weave cloth, is laid on a flat-bed press, a mound of pomace is placed in the center of the cloth, and the four corners are folded over the pomace. Pressing can then take place with pomace neatly contained and easy to handle.

The hand press shown in the photograph is easily made from two boards and a short length of rope. Select $3'\times4''\times1''$ boards of birch, maple, oak, or other strong wood that will not add a foreign flavor to the wine. As shown, the pressing bag filled with pomace is hung from a convenient beam. The

* DuPont registered trademark
† Dow registered trademark

press, like a giant pair of hands on either side of the bag, furnishes pressure to extract the juice.

Several different scales for weighing materials are shown. The common household scale that measures up to twenty-four pounds by ounces is accurate enough for large quantities such as pounds of fruit or sugar. For smaller amounts, a postal scale can be useful. Most laboratory scales that can measure a single gram are fairly expensive, and the beginning wine maker can use the conversion tables in the Appendix to arrive at approximately correct amounts for small quantities of material. A better solution is to try to locate one of the very versatile plastic balances manufactured by the firm Dr. Oetker, in Germany. This balance measures amounts as small as five grams, has scales in both grams and ounces, has a maximum capacity of one pound, and is very accurate and relatively inexpensive. Ask for it at local German delicatessen or imported-food shops.

Scales and balances for measuring sugar, chemicals, and other ingredients. The household scale and large, old-fashioned balance are useful for large quantities, while the two balances in front are used for smaller amounts of materials.

Wine making requires containers of many different sizes and capacities. This requirement is necessary in order that each container be filled as close to the brim as possible, with minimum air space. Each time wine is racked, some dregs remain, and if the wine were replaced in a bottle of the same size, too large an air space would result. This space must be filled with wine of a similar type or the remaining wine must be placed in smaller containers. Glass bottles and jugs are commonly available in the following sizes: 5-gallon, 1-gallon, ½-gallon, quart, ⅕-gallon, pint, and ⅒-gallon. Some demijohns are available in larger sizes, but these, when full, weigh too much to be easily handled, and are both easily broken and expensive. A full 5-gallon bottle weighs about forty-five pounds and is about as much slippery glass as a man can handle with safety. Occasionally demijohns or bottles of odd sizes, such as twenty liters or two liters, may be found. These are a useful supplement to the bottle sizes commonly available and should be treasured.

If possible, wine should be aged in traditional wine bottles with cork stoppers. Screw-top bottles are not satisfactory, particularly for wines of good quality. Pop bottles with crown caps are to be used only in emergencies, and are not safe to use in making champagne. Carbonated soft drinks are generally bottled at pressures ranging from 20 to 40 pounds per square inch, while champagne develops pressures of 55 to 75 pounds per square inch.

Corks have been the traditional bottle stoppers for at least two centuries, some historians claiming they came into general use with bottles in the fifteenth century. They are still preferred for wine that is good enough to age, and contribute not only protection but added flavor to the wine. Bottles with cork stoppers should always be stored on their sides, so the wine can keep the cork moist and expanded. Corks that are allowed to dry out permit air to enter the bottle and offer no protection from deterioration. Corks should be at least 1½ inches long and ¹⁵⁄₁₆ inch in diameter, and of the best

Using the hand corker. The cork has just been driven home by
the plunger. A mallet with a rubber head will often be useful in
seating stubborn corks.

quality available. It is poor economy to buy second-quality
corks, when their cost is so small. Never try to use secondhand
corks. They are a waste of time and effort. When shopping
for store-bought wine, it is a safe practice to patronize mer-
chants that store and display wine bottles on their sides.

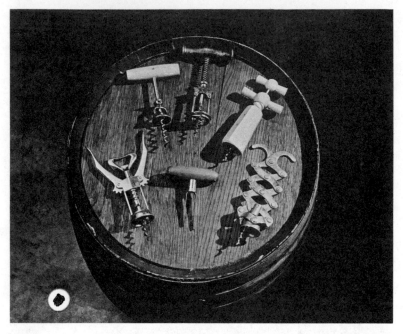

Various bottle openers. The recommended type is in the 2 o'clock position.

Corks in standing bottles can dry out quite rapidly in ordinary shop temperatures, and chances of wine deterioration increase.

Polyethylene stoppers are useful for homemade champagnes, and bottles stopped in this manner need not be stored on the side. They have the advantage of being reusable. However, champagne bottles have narrower necks than do standard wine bottles, so polyethylene stoppers cannot be used for still-wine bottles. Another limitation to the use of plastic stoppers is that they are not impervious to air, so they should not be used for wines that are to be stored for longer than three years.

Wine corks are not tapered, but are made with straight

sides, so a corking machine is required to force them into the necks of bottles. Several different types of corkers are available, but the least expensive is the wooden corking machine that is built somewhat like an old-fashioned popgun. A wood plunger drives the cork through the hollow center of the machine into the neck of the bottle. It is recommended for beginning wine makers.

Cork extractors come in as many forms and varieties as the mind of man can devise. Most consist of a variation on a true corkscrew, which is a spiral of steel around a hollow center. Many are not really screws, but augers, which have solid centers, and are quite useful for pulling the centers out of corks. A corkscrew can be identified by inscrting a toothpick in the hollow center. It is the most useful means of removing corks. Other types employ various techniques for removing corks. One type has parallel steel strips that are forced between the side of the cork and the neck of the bottle. These often work well, but in many cases tend to push the cork into the bottle. Cork removers that operate like hypodermic syringes, and pump either air or carbon dioxide into the space between the top of the wine and the bottom of the cork, are quite frequently advertised. They often raise the cork just enough so the air or gas can escape from around the edges, then move it no farther. Their most serious fault, however, is that if a cork is tightly held in the neck of the bottle, and that bottle has any sort of flaw in the glass, enough pressure can be developed to burst the bottle, sending fragments of glass across the room in an extremely dangerous manner. Documented instances of this sort of accident have prompted me to classify such cork extractors as extremely dangerous and not to be used.

The most reliable cork remover consists of a spiral of steel wire that is designed so that the point enters the cork at the periphery of the spiral. A secondary wood spiral that is turned with another handle slowly and dependably withdraws the imbedded steel spiral and the cork from the bottle.

This completes the list of basic wine making equipment. Not all the items discussed need to be acquired at once— for example, wine should not be bottled and corked until all fermentation has stopped and the wine is perfectly clear; thus corks and corkers are not needed for some time after wine making has started. Pressing bags may be substituted for other types of strainers, and, with a good deal of luck, wine can even be made without a hydrometer or a thermometer. Equipment for more sophisticated or larger-scale wine making efforts will be discussed in a later section. No prices are given for equipment, since they change so rapidly. It is recommended that catalogs and price lists be requested from suppliers listed in the Appendix.

3

Wine Making Yeasts and Chemicals

For many centuries, wine was made by simply crushing grapes or other fruit and allowing nature and the wild yeasts to take over. Some of the finest wines are still made in this manner. The great bulk of wine produced in this traditional method, for lack of a little understanding and a few simple precautions, is the vile, almost undrinkable wine consumed in vast amounts by peasants in all parts of the world.

Thanks to the pioneering work of some of the nineteenth-century scientists, such as Koch and Pasteur, we now understand the reasons why wine spoils, and how to prevent such spoilage. Wine is simply one stage of a cycle that begins with the vine's transformation of water and salts derived from the soil into the neat packages we call grapes, containing sugar, liquid, acids, and flavors. By breaking open these packages and allowing yeasts to work on the contents, we start the process toward becoming wine. Unless the course of this cycle is broken by man's efforts, the step after wine is vinegar, which finally breaks down into water and a few salts, very similar to the original material absorbed by vine roots at the start of the cycle.

Our contribution to this sequence is to provide the most favorable conditions for the change of fruit pulp into wine, and then to prevent any of the subsequent steps from taking place. Traditional methods of making wine have much to offer, simply because they are the result of centuries of observation, practice, trial, and mistake. Coupled with our present understanding of the reasons why these techniques work, they offer the best chance for success.

One of the basic rules for the wine maker to have in the back of his mind at all times is that wines that are not fortified with additional alcohol will spoil when exposed to air. Yeasts require a certain amount of oxygen to grow and function, but the enzymes they produce, which do the actual work of converting sugar to alcohol, need no oxygen from the air in order to function. Vinegar bacilli, on the other hand, cannot grow and reproduce without access to air. This means that one of the wine maker's principal concerns is to assure that the proper, limited amount of air reaches the wine at the correct time, and to prevent air from reaching the wine at other times.

Another responsibility of the wine maker is to provide favorable conditions for wine yeasts to grow and thrive. This involves reducing competition from undesirable yeasts and furnishing a properly balanced diet for the working yeasts. Fortunately, the same ingredients that make the best wine are the favorite food of *Saccharomyces cerevisiae*, var. ellipsoideus, our friend the wine yeast.

Before the wine yeasts can start their work, the wild yeasts present on all fruit should be destroyed. This practice assures that the possibility of off flavors developing from unwanted yeasts will be minimized and that the pure strain of yeasts will be able to get a good start toward active fermentation and overwhelm any wild yeasts that may later find their way into the must. One way to sterilize the must is by heating, and many recipes call for boiling the must for various lengths of time ranging from a few minutes to several hours. While this procedure is quite thorough, it often changes the entire character of the must and converts it from a fresh, fruity-tasting substance to one that tastes more like a plate of preserves. In order to retain most of the delicate flavor of fresh fruit, my recommendation is to simply pour boiling water over the fruit and let it cool. This destroys most of the wild microorganisms without drastically modifying the flavor and fragrance of the material from which the wine is to be made. Boiling water is also useful for extracting maximum flavor from flowers, herbs, and other non-fruit raw materials for wine. It also assures that maximum color and flavor are obtained from berries and Concord grapes.

The second method of eliminating undesirable microorganisms is to add sulfur dioxide to the must. Sulfur dioxide is a colorless gas that mixes readily with water; it has been used in wine making and food preservation for centuries. Second only to salt it is the most universally used food preservative. As in all matters concerning wine making, moderation in its use is required. Applied in excessive quantities, the flavor of the sulfur is noticed in finished wine and can spoil the pleasure and digestion of the consumer. When used with discretion, it can be beneficial and reduce chances of spoilage to a minimum. A dosage of six ounces of potassium metabisulfite per ton of grapes eliminates 99.9 per cent of the cells of active microorganisms in normal musts. Translated to home wine making amounts, this is about three grams of potassium metabisulfite for five gallons of must. For smaller ferments, potassium metabisulfite is packaged in a form called Campden tablets, each of which contains seven grains and is adequate for one gallon of wine. Campden tablets can be obtained from most amateur wine making supply houses, and should be crushed and dissolved in a little water before being added to the must. The portions given above are to be used for musts made of sound, ripe fruit that has a good acid balance.

Sulfur dioxide, the active ingredient released by potassium metabisulfite and Campden tablets, is also sold in large cylinders for wineries, or is released when sulfur wicks or "candles" are burned in barrels and vats to sterilize them, providing protection for wine they will contain. Sulfur wicks have two serious defects: (1) they leave residues that can be transformed to hydrogen sulfide by yeasts, and (2) it is almost impossible to measure and control the amount of sulfur dioxide produced.

Amateur wine makers will find potassium metabisulfite or Campden tablets the most reliable and convenient form of sulfur dioxide. Potassium metabisulfite, which releases approximately 50 per cent of free sulfur dioxide, is preferred over sodium bisulfite, suggested or recommended in some books. Sodium bisulfite may be a trifle less expensive, and be quite as efficient when used in amateur wine making, but it is not always reliable in composition and may contain undesirable amounts of heavy metals.

Potassium metabisulfite not only eliminates wild yeasts and other microorganisms in the must, but reduces browning of

Crushing grapes with traditional twin-roller crusher.

freshly crushed fruit, increases fixed acidity, increases the color of many red wines having good total acidity, reduces free (acetic) acidity, and promotes better fermentation, resulting in generally sounder wines.

As mentioned earlier, excessive use of potassium metabisulfite tends to give wine an unpleasant taste, inhibits natural aging, and may lead to turbid wines. Only minimum quantities of potassium metabisulfite should be added to the wine, depending upon such factors as temperature of the must, maturity of the fruit, and its freedom from bruises, mold, and damage. For fruit that is cool, sound, and ripe, with good acid content, and that will be fermented at low temperatures, as little as 1.5 grams of potassium metabisulfite may be used for each five gallons of must. For riper fruit, having less acid, where fermentation will take place about 70° F, the figure given earlier, of three grams per five gallons, is adequate. The absolute maximum allowable is one gram per gallon.

For sterilizing fruit by pouring boiling water over it, the fruit should be left whole until the water has cooled. When potassium metabisulfite is employed, it should be dissolved in a little water and the solution added to the freshly crushed fruit, stirred, and adequately mixed into the must. This permits the anti-oxidant and clarifying properties of the potassium metabisulfite solution to improve the quality of the must.

After a few hours, the sterilizing effect of potassium metabisulfite is reduced, particularly in its effects on yeast. At this time the active pure wine yeast can be added with confidence that nearly perfect fermentation will result.

The primary yeast food is sugar, either that found naturally in fruit, or store-bought sugar added by the wine maker to supplement the fruit's natural store. Most wine yeasts can utilize sugar concentrations up to about 30 per cent of the total volume. That amount of sugar, if fermented to dryness, will result in approximately 15 per cent alcohol. Wines usually taste better and are more pleasant to drink if they are somewhat less alcoholic, so wine makers of experience usually aim for dry table wines containing about 12 per cent alcohol. Wines can be made that have less alcohol, but they are generally unstable, do not age gracefully, and must be consumed while they are young.

Wines with somewhat more sugar than the yeasts can convert are classified as medium, or medium-dry, wines, while those with larger amounts of unconverted, excess sugar are known as sweet wines. The scale on page 32 shows the approximate hydrometer readings associated with each type of wine. By taking a hydrometer reading of the juice from which the wine will be made, one obtains a basis for determining the amount of sugar that must be added to produce the type of wine desired. If the must contains more sugar than is wanted, water may be added until the proper sugar content is obtained. In most municipalities, water from the kitchen faucet may be used without previous boiling. In communities where large amounts of chlorine are used, it is preferred to boil the water and let it cool before adding it to the must. Some localities are troubled with water that contains a high percentage of iron or other unwanted minerals. In such places, it is probably best to rely on bottled water for any necessary additions to the wine.

If additional sugar is required, a general rule to remember is that to raise a gallon of must 1° Balling, approximately ⅛ pound of sugar is needed. For example, if a wine maker wishes to produce a medium wine containing about 14 per cent alcohol with residual sugar of about 4 per cent, then he will want his total Balling measurement to be 32°. If the fresh must measures 18° Balling, then a total of fourteen ⅛ pounds, or 1¾ pounds, of sugar should be added to each gallon of must.

If that amount of sugar were to be added all at once, there is danger that the yeasts would be overwhelmed and their activity reduced or even stopped completely. To avoid this difficulty, sugar is added in two installments, so the fermentation need never be interrupted or stopped. An even better method is to remove part of the liquid and melt half of the sugar in it, heating it just enough so the sugar is entirely dissolved and a syrup results. When the syrup is cool, it may be returned to the vat, where it will mix very readily with the must and not be deposited at the bottom of the fermentation vat.

Empirical methods of making wine, techniques that were passed along from wine maker to wine maker and were successful even though the reasons why they worked were not understood, were almost universally practiced prior to the middle of the nineteenth century. Gradually, understanding of the processes that took place during the transformation of juice into wine became more general and was applied in a rational manner. The empirical approach is still with us, however, and sometimes results in suggestions that can confuse those who do not understand the way things really work. For example, you will find books written for amateur wine makers that insist the best sugar for wine making is pure cane sugar, and that beet sugar makes inferior wine. Other authors recommend that cane or beet sugar must first be changed to invert sugar before a satisfactory wine can be made. These statements should be approached with the understanding that sucrose, a disaccharide, with the chemical formula $C_{12}H_{22}O_{11}$, is identified as cane sugar, beet sugar, or maple sugar, according to the source from which it originated, and when refined, has the same chemical and molecular structure no matter what the source. Invert sugar is an optical isomer of sucrose, and differs in structure and composition only in that it displaces a beam of polarized light in the opposite direction from that of sucrose.

Invert sugar is made by adding water and acid or lemon juice to sucrose and heating until the sugar dissolves. Either sucrose or its optical isomer, invert sugar, is immediately hydrolized into fructose ($C_6H_{12}O_6$) (levulose) and its isomer glucose ($C_6H_{12}O_6$), when added to the must.

It appears obvious that for our wine making purposes we can use the handiest, least expensive, store-bought sugar and be quite sure that as far as sugar is concerned, our wine will be as good as that made with more expensive and less readily available forms.

Although most of us who practice the art like to think of ourselves as wine makers, this is really not the case. The true wine makers are the yeasts that manufacture the enzymes that do the actual conversion of sugar into alcohol. This conversion is not a simple process, but, according to Amerine and Joslyn, the glucose molecule passes anaerobically through twelve stable intermediate stages before the alcohol and carbon dioxide are finally produced. Between three and eight organic enzymes, approximately twenty and possibly more enzyme proteins, and five inorganic catalytic materials are provided by the yeast cells during the fermentation process. It may be seen that the end result is an extremely complex substance.

The yeasts responsible for this activity are single-celled plants called *Saccharomyces cerevisiae*, var. ellipsoideus. While a number of other types of yeasts are commonly found in fermenting musts that have not been sterilized and inoculated with pure strains, they are undesirable, giving unexpected and sometimes unpleasant results. It is well to take advantage of the easy availability of pure cultures of wine yeasts to assure reliable fermentation.

The amateur wine maker must select between the viewpoints of the old-fashioned, rough and ready "spread a square of baker's yeast on toast and float it on the wine" school, and the typical German yeast manufacturer who can provide a different strain of yeast for every type of wine produced along the Rhine. There is no doubt that certain yeasts will give different wine flavors, even when the same grapes are used. It is doubtful, however, that beyond assuring rapid and vigorous fermentation and elimination of spoilage and off flavors, that more should be expected from pure yeasts. It can be guaran-

Hand-operated, homemade crusher/stemmer made entirely of poly-vinyl-chloride sheet and pipe. Note plastic sheeting used to funnel must into fermentation vat, and stems being ejected from end of pipe.

teed without reservation that even the most select yeast cannot make Schloss Johannisberg out of Thompson seedless grapes. Fortunately the amateur wine maker is not hampered by economic restraints, and can afford to experiment. It might be interesting to divide batches of must into several ferments, starting each with a different strain of yeast.

In addition to the familiar moist cakes of baker's yeast that, in a pinch, can be used for wine making, pure yeasts are generally available in three different forms: a liquid, generally sold in small, sealed plastic bottles; an agar slant, also generally sold in bottles; and dry active wine yeast, available in small, sealed foil packages. The dry yeast needs only to be opened and sprinkled on the surface of the must to initiate fermentation. Depositing the entire contents of the package on one spot is recommended, and allowing the colony to develop for several hours before stirring, gives best results.

Bottled wine yeasts in liquid media do not contain enough yeast organisms to initiate rapid, vigorous fermentation in themselves but must be amplified by an intermediate step known as a "starter." Yeast starters are developed either from agar slants or bottles of liquid yeast in the following manner:

—Use a sterile pint bottle.
—Fill half full of sterile fruit juice. This may be either freshly pressed and boiled or a commercial pasteurized fruit juice with no preservatives.
—Add 1 tsp sugar.
—Add juice of half a lemon.
—Shake bottle of liquid yeast and add to cool juice.
—Plug bottle neck with cotton wool.
—Set aside for two to three days until actively fermenting.
—Add to must that has been sulfited four hours earlier.

Using a liquid yeast starter requires planning several days in advance of the beginning of fermentation. If the exact time that fruit will be ready for crushing is known, starters can be prepared for use when maximum yeast activity is reached.

On the other hand, if an unexpected gift of wine making material arrives, it is more practical to use dry wine yeast, which needs no preparation. It is prudent to keep a package or two of dry wine yeast on hand for any such fortunate emergencies.

Yeasts, like all other plants and most living creatures, function best when adequately nourished with a proper diet, which consists not only of carbohydrates (sugar), but minerals as well. Many of the non-grape substances from which wines are made are quite deficient in minerals, so it is wise to add some nourishment to assure healthy fermentation of such materials. Most nutrients are in the form of ammonium salts, but some proprietary compounds may contain potassium and phosphates as well. There appears to be a direct relationship between the nitrogen content of the must and the speed of fermentation.

Almost all grapes contain sufficient nutrients for rapid and complete fermentation. They can be added to other wines, either as fresh grapes in season or as raisins, to provide sufficient yeast nutrients to wine materials such as roots, herbs, and flowers, which benefit from addition of such nutritive substances. In instances in which addition of nutrients is indicated, it is generally preferred to add chopped raisins to the other ingredients rather than pure chemical salts such as ammonium phosphate, ammonium chloride, or other combinations of chemicals sold as proprietary yeast nutrients.

A number of materials that otherwise make interesting wines are deficient, or completely lacking, in acids. This tends to result in flat, insipid-tasting wines. To correct non-acid musts, acid is added in sufficient amounts to improve taste. This addition also promotes development and growth of yeasts and reduces the chances of undesirable microorganisms taking over during fermentation. Proper acid balance also increases the color of red wines and reduces browning of white wines.

Several different acids are found in various fruits, the

most commonly met with being citric, in citrus fruits; malic, in apples; and tannic, in grapes. Acids generally found in grape wines include those mentioned above plus tartaric, lactic, succinic, sulfurous, and carbonic. A number of others can develop during both healthy and spoiled fermentations, but these are of less importance than those mentioned above. Ordinarily, acid-deficient wines are improved by the addition of citric, malic, or tannic acid, or a combination of these three. It is almost impossible to tell by taste alone whether a must has sufficient acid to produce a well-balanced wine. For example, a high-acid fruit containing 25 per cent sugar will taste quite sweet, with the unfermented sugar covering up the acid in the must. Conversely, a low-acid, low-sugar must can taste quite sour. When the necessary amount of sugar is added to such musts, there is not enough acid to properly balance the must for active, healthy fermentation and a sound wine. The only reliable test for acid content of musts or wine is titration. This is more complicated than testing for sugar and involves neutralizing the acid in a specific amount of wine by a standard alkaline solution. Testing for acid is accomplished in the following way: In 1 wine bottle (75 cl) of distilled water, place 3 grams of anhydrous (dry) sodium hydroxide. Shake well from time to time, allowing all of the sodium hydroxide to dissolve. (Note that French wine bottles contain 75 cl, while American wine bottles have slightly larger capacity, 25.6 ounces, which is equivalent to 75.699 cl. If an American wine bottle is used for measuring the water, a small amount less should be used.) This will give a 0.1 normal solution of sodium hydroxide. If anhydrous sodium hydroxide is not readily available, the reliable neighborhood pharmacist will make up a 0.1 N solution. CAUTION! sodium hydroxide is extremely caustic and should be handled with respect, but never with *bare* hands. The bottle in which the solution is made should not be used for any other purpose and should be kept in a safe place. A solution of phenolphthalein (1 gram dry phenolphthalein in 100 cc neutral alcohol) or some litmus paper will also be needed. Either of these can be obtained from the pharmacy.

Equipment necessary for testing will be:

burette, 50 cc or ml graduated to $\frac{1}{10}$ cc or ml
stand, for holding the burette
medicine dropper
porcelain dish 7–8″ in diameter
glass stirring rod
graduated cylinder or pipette.

Steps in testing are:

(1) Fill the burette to the zero mark with the .1 N sodium hydroxide solution, being sure that the lowest part of the meniscus is at the zero line.

(2) Shake the sample of must or wine to be tested for about one minute to remove any carbon dioxide. Allow gas to escape, and repeat. If the CO_2 were not removed, as an acid it would change the values obtained in the test.

(3) Add 250–300 ml distilled or boiled water to the porcelain dish. To this, add a medicine dropper full of the phenolphthalein solution and stir well. If litmus paper is used, the water may be omitted, and papers of approximately 1 inch square may be used.

(4) Add enough of the .1 N sodium hydroxide solution (not from the burette) to obtain a definite pink color in the porcelain dish containing water and phenolphthalein. Stir the mixture thoroughly.

(5) Add 10 ml of the must or wine that is to be tested. If a deep-red wine is being tested, add only 5 ml.

(6) Run the sodium hydroxide solution from the burette into the sample in the porcelain dish, stirring constantly with the glass stirring rod. When a distinct pink color has been obtained, shut off the stopcock of the burette.

(7) Divide the number of milliliters of sodium hydroxide

solution taken from the burette by the number of milliliters of the sample of wine or must used. Multiply the number obtained by 7.5 to learn the acid content of the must expressed in grams tartaric per liter. To obtain the number of grams per liter of citric acid in berry and fruit wines, the number obtained by dividing the number of milliliters of sodium hydroxide by the number of milliliters of the sample should be multiplied by a factor of 7, while that number should be multiplied by a factor of 6.7 to obtain the amount of malic acid in apple wine or must.

Addition of acid to musts generally improves most dry wines and can be routinely included as part of the wine making process after the test for acid has been made. Sweet wines need less acid than do dry wines, which should contain between 0.6 per cent and 0.8 per cent of acid expressed in grams tartaric before fermentation. Tannic acid added to grape musts insures rapid, trouble-free fermentation and a smoother wine when it is finished.

Sorbic acid is used in commercial wineries to prevent multiplication of yeasts, especially in unfortified, naturally sweet wines. However, for best results it should be used in conjunction with, rather than as a substitute for, sulfur dioxide. Sorbic acid tends to produce off odors, and as a result cannot be recommended for use with wines of superior quality.

Calcium carbonate (precipitated chalk) is added to some wines to reduce high levels of fixed acids. It is often suggested for rhubarb wine. Chalk should be added to the must near the end of fermentation at the rate of about three teaspoons per gallon, and allowed to stand for four days, then racked, with citric acid added to replace the oxalic acid extracted from the rhubarb. Other high-acid wines, made from such fruits as gooseberries and limes, are best neutralized by simply adding water or blending with low-acid wines. This avoids the changes in taste encountered in using calcium carbonate.

Close-up of the combination crusher/press, showing hopper and corrugated rollers for crushing grapes.

Enzymes are proteins that act as catalysts. They are formed by living cells to promote specific reactions to various substances used by those cells. Enzymes differ from inorganic catalysts in that their action is extremely specific and depends upon precise combinations of temperature, degree of acidity or alkalinity, and the presence of other activators or inhibitors. Many thousands of different enzymes are created by various organisms, and large numbers can be expected in a fluid as complex as wine. Amateur wine makers are most concerned with yeast-manufactured enzymes, which convert sugars into alcohol, and pectolytic enzymes, which destroy the pectins that cause haze in the wine. Pectolytic enzymes are used to increase the yield of juice and clarity of wine. These enzymes are available in standard strengths—5:1 and 10:1. Standard-strength enzymes are mixed with freshly crushed fruit at the rate of four grams per gallon. Enzyme strengths of 5:1 and 10:1 should be used in proportionally smaller amounts. The package containing the pectolytic enzyme should have the strength plainly shown or have adequate directions for use.

All the cautions previously mentioned concerning low fermentation temperatures, proper acid content, and thorough mixing of musts are applicable primarily because of their influence on enzyme activity and performance. These desirable conditions also assist in clarifying wine both when the wine clears itself, as most normal, healthy wines tend to do, and also when the help of clarifying agents is needed. Many different materials have been used to make wines clear; among these are: albumen, milk, gelatin, isinglass, blood, lime, plaster of Paris, gum arabic, metal salts, clay, and hot stones. Most of these form a mechanical combination with the turbid particles, then sink to the bottom of the container. Other wine-clearing agents change the chemical nature or the electrical charge of the clouds of particles, causing them to be deposited. The traditional method for determining when wine is clear enough to bottle is to place a lighted candle close to the jug containing the wine, observing the candle flame from the opposite side. If the flame appears perfectly visible, clearly outlined, and undistorted, the wine is ready. Another useful technique, especially in dark cellars, is to shine the narrow beam of a flashlight through the wine, observing from a 90° angle. Any indication of the flashlight beam passing through the wine is evidence that further clarification, either natural or induced, is needed before bottling.

Natural, organic fining materials in common use are albumen, casein, gelatin, and isinglass. Most of these rely on their combining with tannin in the wine to effect clarification. For that reason it is generally necessary to add tannin to white wines at the rate of ½ gram per gallon twenty-four hours before fining with these materials. Exceptions to this rule of thumb are such high-tannin whites wines as those made from grapefruit and pears. Organic fining materials are used in the following ways:

Albumen Beat the white of one egg and a pinch of salt in 1 bottle of wine until frothy. Mix well with the wine, to which tannin was added twenty-four hours earlier. One egg white will clear up to ten gallons of wine. For smaller amounts of wine, use proportionally less egg white. The wine with the egg white should stand quietly for two to three weeks. When clear, rack and bottle.

Gelatin Use the finest obtainable gelatin (unflavored, granulated food gelatin is handy). Dissolve in 1 cup warm water, and add to 1 bottle wine. When thoroughly dissolved in the wine, mix with the remaining tannin-treated wine. Allow to clear; then rack and bottle.

Isinglass Isinglass is a fish gelatin made from sturgeon. It may be possible to obtain from large chemical supply houses or from some of the better-supplied wine materials stores. The required amount of sheet isinglass is soaked in wine for twenty-four hours; then the wine and the isinglass are disintegrated in a blender. Isinglass can be added to tannin-treated wine in the same manner as described for albumen and gelatin.

Casein Wine to be fined with casein should have about half as much tannin added before fining as recommended for wines treated with albumen, gelatin, or isinglass. If dry casein is used, it should be made up in the following manner: Add ¼ tsp sodium bicarbonate to 1 cup water; dissolve casein in this alkaline solution in the proportion of ½ gram per gallon of wine to be treated. When the casein is completely dissolved, add to the wine, stir well, and allow to settle. In an emergency, instant non-fat dry milk powder may be substituted for the casein. Sodium bicarbonate is not necessary for the instant dry milk.

All the above fining agents tend to decolorize wine, so that red wines may be lighter in color after treatment. It is usually not necessary to add tannin to red grape wines being treated, but red wines from most other fruit, except elderberries and currants, can benefit from addition of tannin before fining. As with other cellar operations, the wine should be as little exposed to air as possible, remain cool, and be kept at a stable temperature. If wines treated with these materials remain cloudy after a month, they may possibly be clarified by treatment with bentonite.

Bentonite   Bentonite is a clay, usually derived from volcanic ash, that has the property of expanding in water to many times its original volume. For fining wine it is used as follows: Add dry bentonite to a wine bottle (75 cl) of water at the rate of 1.5 grams per gallon of wine to be treated. It is best to mix the bentonite and water with an electric mixer for about three minutes. Allow mixture to stand overnight; then add to wine, mixing completely, but with minimum aeration of the wine. Allow the tightly stoppered wine to settle in a cool place for two to three weeks, then rack and bottle. Bentonite leaves more sediment than the other materials discussed, so the lees may be poured into a smaller container, stoppered, and allowed to go through a further settling period.

Sparkalloid   Sparkalloid is a proprietary polysaccharide clarifying agent used in commercial wineries. It has the disadvantage for home wine makers that it must be boiled for half an hour and kept hot until used. It may be possible to locate the newer, cold-mix Sparkalloid, which eliminates the bother of using a hot mixture.

Asbestos Asbestos is an effective filtering agent, and when carefully and properly handled, it can be useful in stubborn cases of turbidity. Unfortunately, open filtration of wine permits too much air to mix with the wine, and for that reason is not recommended. Wineries use special filters, which are sealed and do not expose wine to the air. Asbestos is an extremely dangerous material to use, because if its very fine, inert fibers are ingested or breathed into the lungs, trouble in later years is almost certain to result. In commercial wineries special silk bags are (or should be) used to remove any stray asbestos fibers from filtered wines. I recommend that home wine makers stay away from asbestos.

Wood Chips Beechwood chips have for years been used to clarify both beer and wine by *adsorption*; that is, the wood chips tend to attract and concentrate on their surfaces the particles that cause haze. Most haze particles are colloids that have like electrical charges on their surfaces, so they tend to repel each other and keep floating around in the wine instead of being deposited. Wood chips present a large surface that attracts the colloidal particles and helps to clear the wine. Beechwood has a neutral taste and contributes no foreign flavor to the wine. Oak chips, on the other hand, impart a decided taste of oak to the wine, and care must be exercised that the wine is not allowed to become excessively "oaky." Oak chips can be prepared by shaving a debarked piece of oakwood with a plane or a draw knife. The chips are then placed in a pan and allowed to come to a boil two times. The water is poured off, and about 1 gram of the sterile chips are added to each gallon of wine.

Medium wines such as sherries, natural sweet wines such as Barsac and sauternes, and fortified sweet wines such as port, Malaga, and Marsala are all produced by different techniques. For natural sweet wines of the Sauternes and the Hungarian Tokay types, grapes are harvested very late in the season, when natural moisture has evaporated and the remaining pulp contains concentrated sugars. These grapes are fermented in the usual manner, with alcohol content limited to 12–14 per cent. Fortified sweet wines such as port, Madeira, and Malaga have had their fermentation stopped by the addition of brandy before all of the sugar contained in the grapes could be converted to alcohol. These wines may, with their added brandy, contain between 20 and 25 per cent alcohol, depending upon the desires of the wine maker.

Amateur wine makers who wish to experiment with sweet wines should begin with fortified wines. With such wines the fermentation may be interrupted at any degree of sweetness desired by adding sufficient brandy, vodka, or ethyl alcohol to raise the total alcohol content to about 20 per cent by volume. Adding brandy, as is customary with port, sherry, Madeira, Marsala, and other fortified wines, is a problem for home wine makers because of the difficulty of obtaining the kind of neutral-tasting, high-proof brandy used for commercial fortification. Beverage brandy usually imparts a distinct taste to the wine, and should be tried in small amounts before fortifying an entire batch. For wines made from materials other than grapes, a good, neutral-tasting vodka is an acceptable means of fortification. If a source of pure potable ethyl alcohol is available, it too can be used for fortification.

A formula known as the Pearson square is a useful way to determine the amount of alcohol to be added to obtain a preselected percentage. The Pearson square is shown below:

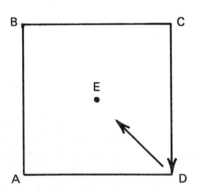

A=percentage of alcohol by volume (not proof) of fortifying spirit.

B=alcohol content of wine to be fortified.

C=difference between alcohol in spirit (A) and alcohol desired in wine (E).

D=difference between alcohol in wine (B) and alcohol desired in wine (E).

E=alcohol content desired.

For example, if we have a wine (B) of 10 per cent alcohol that we want to make into a 20 per cent wine, and brandy that has 45 per cent alcohol (90° proof), then we take the difference between the alcohol content of the wine (B) and the alcohol desired (E)—10 per cent—and the difference between the alcohol in the spirit (A) and the desired alcohol in the wine (E), which is 25 per cent (45 −20). That means that to twenty-five parts of wine we add ten parts of brandy.

We have discussed most of the materials necessary for home wine making. Many other proprietary products are used in commercial wine production. Most of these require special techniques and apparatus and are primarily designed to give a resulting product of standard sparkling clarity and purity. Home wine makers need not try to meet the fanatical American commercial goal of sparkling-clear wines that never throw a deposit. Deposit of sediment during maturing is an accepted result of the aging process in European wines and should be considered in the same way by amateur wine makers.

4

Equipment for Advanced Wine Makers

In the first section, equipment necessary for beginning wine making projects was discussed. Such equipment is perfectly adequate for anyone whose largest batch of wine will be less than twenty to twenty-five gallons.

After a period of learning and trial, most wine makers find that it is almost as much trouble to make wine in small quantities as to make larger amounts. By the time the five-gallon ferment has been racked twice or three times, sampled often enough to check progress, and submitted to a few friends for evaluation, precious little remains to age and be enjoyed at maturity. A resolution is eventually made to increase the wine production to allow laying down of enough wine to allow some to reach the golden years.

A decision of this sort requires foresight and planning. The wine maker who resolves to make his full legal allotment of two hundred gallons annually must take into account the following considerations:

1. Can the family kitchen still be used, or will the clutter and mess drive the wife up the wall and bring an immediate return of Prohibition?

2. Is there sufficient space to process and store two hundred gallons of wine?

3. Will the entire amount be made at one time, as would

be indicated if grape wine is to be made, or will several different wines be made at various times?

4. Assuming that two hundred gallons of grape wine are to be made, about 2,500 pounds of grapes will be required. This is equivalent to half a hundred 50-pound boxes, or about a hundred lug boxes of grapes.

a. How will these grapes be transported, and will the grower allow use of his boxes during the busy harvest season or will other containers need to be furnished?

b. When the grapes arrive, can they be stored until processed, or must they be crushed immediately?

c. Is there enough fermentation-vat capacity to accept 2,500 pounds of grapes and the cap that will be formed? (About three hundred gallons of capacity will be necessary.)

d. Can an even, cool temperature be maintained during primary and secondary fermentation?

e. Will there be enough manpower available to help process the grapes?

If the answers to all these questions are affirmative, or at least no serious problems arise, necessary equipment can be obtained.

The neatest and least cumbersome fermentation vat for this amount of wine is a polyethylene tank with cover, that has a capacity of three hundred gallons. Space required will be about forty-two inches in diameter and sixty-one inches in height. A vat of this size is simplest to use, store, and keep clean for future wine making. Its disadvantages are that it costs between $175 and $200, and that it is really too large for smaller vintages. Other solutions to the problem, in order of their utility and advantages, are:

(1) Polyethylene trash containers of 32 to 45 gallon capacity. These should be purchased with covers; they range in price from about $8 to $15 each. About ten 32-gallon containers will be needed for 2,500 pounds of grapes.

(2) Fifty-five-gallon steel drums with heavy-gauge polyeth-

ylene liners. Used drums are available at about $4 each, and polyethylene liners are available from some dealers in barrels and from a few wine supply stores. Such liners cost about a dollar each, and, if carefully treated, will protect the must during fermentation. One word of caution! In punching down the cap and stirring the must, great care should be exercised to prevent holes from being torn in the liner. The stirring paddle should have well-rounded edges, and it is a good idea to forget about scraping skins and debris from the sides of the vat.

(3) Used fermentation vats are available in some parts of the country. These are ordinarily made of oak or redwood and

Traditional basket press. The pressed juice is allowed to undergo secondary fermentation in the barrel to give added oak flavoring to the wine.

have become available because they are no longer being used by their original owners. A good source for this kind of container, or indeed any kind of wine making equipment, is an Italian family in which the first generation made wine but the younger people are no longer interested. Any equipment that is not new should always be examined very carefully before purchase, to make certain that no irreversible damage has been done to the wood. Termites and wood borers enter through very small holes, then proceed to eat the heart out of the wood, leaving merely a shell. Exploratory prodding with the blade of a knife will tell if the wood is sound. If barrels or vats are found to be solid, they should be cleaned and prepared as described below. Musty or sour-smelling casks or vats require much patient rehabilitation effort, and even then there is no guarantee that offensive odors can be permanently removed.

(4) Used 50-gallon whiskey, rum, or brandy barrels can be used as primary fermenters. In preparation, the barrel should be stood on end and the top two hoops driven off with a cold chisel and hammer. As the staves loosen, the head will drop into the barrel, although it may need some pushing down on one side, so that when it is at right angles to its normal position it can most easily be removed. After the head has been put aside, the hoops should be replaced and driven home. Next, careful examination should be made with eyes, nose, and a good flashlight or drop light. Observe these cautions:

—Be sure the barrels are sound and have no leaky staves or heads.

—Make certain the barrels have not been used for pickling, vinegar, or worse. If they smell unpleasant, grow strawberries in them. If they have traces of whiskey or brandy, they may be used if properly treated. Any other odor should be suspect and the barrel discarded.

—Make sure the barrels are free from mold and decay and have no wormholes.

—Be very certain that time and patience are available to

store the barrels properly during the time they are not in use.

If the barrel to be used for a fermentation vat has been charred, it should be scraped with an old hoe that has been ground to the proper shape to fit the curvature of the barrel surface. It may also be brushed with a steel wire brush to remove loose particles of charred oak. After this debris has been removed, wash the barrel thoroughly with a stream of cold water, then scrub with the following solution:

To 1 gallon hot water add 1 ounce lye and 9 ounces sal soda. Stir well, and while hot, scrub the inside of the barrel, making sure that none of the hot solution gets on clothes or skin, or in the eyes. Rinse the barrel thoroughly with hot water, empty, and run the barrel full of cold water. Add 1 cup Clorox to the water in the barrel, stir thoroughly, then rinse well with cold water. Drain completely, and allow to dry for at least twenty-four hours.

When the barrel is completely dry, paint the inside with paraffin, melting the wax in a clean can or an old pot. Brush the paraffin onto the wood with a cheap, new brush. When the paraffin is cold, the barrel may be used as a fermentation vat.

(5) New oak or redwood vats are a considerable investment. For example, new oak barrels with capacity of 50 to 100 gallons cost between $75 and $100 each. This represents a large investment for a capacity of three hundred gallons. The cost of new cooperage should be compared with the price of used whiskey or brandy barrels at about $15. An investment in new oak barrels will be more advantageous if they are used for aging rather than fermenting wines.

With adequate primary fermentation capacity arranged for, a means for crushing grapes is the next objective. Crushing by hand, mashing with a wood pestle, and even stomping out the vintage under foot are inadequate methods for handling quantities as large as 2,500 pounds. The familiar single- or two-roller crushers are the most readily available means for crushing grapes and other berries. Similar machines with

Crusher and basket press mounted on a single chassis. These combination units are compact and efficient for home wineries, and diligent search may unearth one.

toothed rollers are used for shredding such fruit as apples, pears, and quinces. They may be used for apricots, plums, peaches, etc. if the stones are removed first.

Single-roller crushers are made with sharp teeth cut into the roller. These pass between other teeth mounted on the throat of the hopper. Grapes are caught between the fixed and the rotating teeth, ground up, and fall into the container below. The disadvantage of the single-roller crusher is that the stems tend to be chopped and added to the must, and, when they are in small pieces, become difficult to remove.

Double-roller crushers have a pair of rollers, either smooth or corrugated, that rotate toward each other, crushing the grapes in between. Rollers are ordinarily adjustable so that enough space is allowed for the seeds to pass through undamaged while all the fruit is crushed. Grape seeds contain bitter substances that are released when the seeds are crushed and can seriously mar the flavor of the wine. Crushers of this

Close-up of the combination crusher/press, showing detail of the press. The four extrusions on the wheel allow a two-by-four to be used to increase leverage and pressure.

type can be either hand or motor operated, and are adequate for any quantity of grapes the home wine maker will process.

Most wineries look for the earliest maturity possible for the wines they produce, and for this reason practice removal of stems prior to fermentation of red wines. White wines are pressed before fermenting, and stems are not removed from the grapes. While dry woody stems make very little difference in the tannin content of the wine, green stems contribute a considerable amount of tannin when allowed to remain with the fermenting must. Such wines need a long period of aging before the wine becomes drinkable. On the other hand, some varieties of grapes have less than enough tannin in their skins to make sound wines, and benefit from incorporation of stems in the must. A good compromise for the home wine maker is to remove all but about 25 per cent of the stems when red wine is being made.

Hand removal of the stems before crushing is a tedious task, and after crushing, a messy one. The simplest way to separate stems is to make a device similar to that shown in the accompanying photograph. This consists of a wood panel made from a hard, non-splintering, neutral-flavored wood, such as birch, beech, poplar, or maple, approximately twenty-four inches square. A frame that is two to three inches wide surrounds the panel and prevents grapes from falling off the edges. In the panel are drilled a series of 1-inch holes on 3-inch centers. These holes should be chamfered, to prevent the edges from splintering. The device is placed on top of the fermenting vat, and a bunch of grapes is taken in each hand. The grapes are rubbed against the board so they are crushed and fall through the holes while the stems remain on top and can be separated. This method may seem primitive, but it is in current use at such wineries as Château Pichon-Longueville (Baron), Château Latour, and Château Mouton-Rothschild, each of which makes more than eighty thousand bottles of wine a year, and which are pretty good examples to follow.

If a roller-type crusher is used, a framework of similar size

Crushing and stemming grapes with a hand crusher/stemmer board.

made of redwood with $\frac{1}{16}$-inch holes drilled an inch apart around all four sides approximately 1½ inches from the bottom edge is strung with heavy (at least 40-pound-test) monofilament fishline. The line is threaded and woven to form a grid that will catch the stems as they drop from the crusher while the grapes fall through to the container below. The grid is placed on the edges of the fermentation vat, and the crusher is placed on top of the grid frame. If the vat has a very large opening, the grid frame can be suspended below the crusher.

A good press is the most expensive piece of equipment the home wine maker will require. Two types of press are in common use for small operations: the traditional basket press and the rack press. Both types work well and are efficient ex-

Close-up of hand crusher/stemmer in operation. Grapes are crushed on the board and fall through the holes into the vat, while the stems remain on the board and can be removed.

tractors of juice. Basket presses are primarily used for grapes, while rack presses are commonly employed to extract juice from apples. Basket presses are so called because the grapes are contained in a circle of vertical oak staves supported by metal rings surrounding a central screw, which may rise from the bottom of the press or be suspended over the basket by a framework. If the screw is fastened to the bottom of the basket area, it naturally comes in contact with both grapes and wine, and unless protected by a coating of petroleum jelly or painted with epoxy, will contaminate the must.

Some basket presses are made with the screw set in a frame above the basket. This arrangement allows use of press cloths or press bags when desired, and reduces the possibility of iron contamination of the wine.

Rack presses consist of a framework like that of the basket presses with the screw on the top frame. The bottom of the frame supports a solid flat plate, which in turn has a rectangular container about four inches deep that holds the pressed juice and allows it to flow out through a faucet or a spigot. The juice container can be a plastic dishpan, carrying tray, or other polyethylene basin of the proper size to fit in the frame of the press. If no plastic basin of the proper size is available, one can be made of wood lined with paraffin to make a liquid-tight receptacle for the juice. The press is loaded in the following manner: A rack made of oak slats is placed in the bottom. On this is spread a pressing cloth made of plastic window screen or loosely woven cotton, nylon, or Saran fabric. The fruit to be pressed is heaped in the center of the cloth. When enough fruit pulp is placed to form a mass two to three inches thick and slightly smaller than the rack, the corners of the cloth are folded over the top of the fruit to entirely contain it. Another rack is placed on top of the "cheese" formed in this manner. A second pressing cloth is positioned on top of the second rack and the process of making a cheese is repeated. For small home presses, three or four cheeses may be stacked before pressing begins. In commercial operations rack presses capable of holding as many as fifteen to twenty cheeses are loaded before the hydraulic presses are operated. Rack presses are the most useful and versatile design for home wine makers, since they can be used for many different kinds of fruit that basket presses handle less efficiently or not at all. In addition, they can easily be constructed by the home craftsman in such a way as to eliminate any metal contamination of the wine—a feature almost impossible with conventional basket presses.

Plans for a simple rack press are shown below. This press has the following bill of materials:

1 sheet 4×8' marine-grade ¾" plywood
1 polyethylene tray approx. 25×17×8" deep
1 ton-and-a-half hydraulic jack or equivalent
4 oak racks to fit in polyethylene tray
20 carriage bolts with washers (⅜×4")
30 twelvepenny common nails

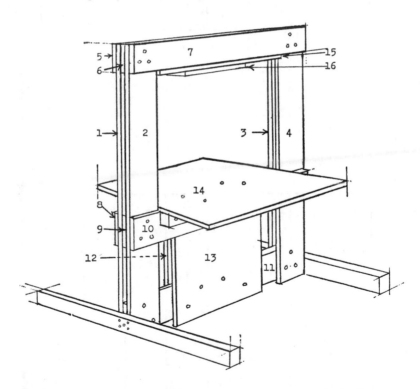

FIGURE 1: *Drawing of simple frame for rack press with platform for plastic tray. This press can be used with hydraulic jack for applying pressure.*

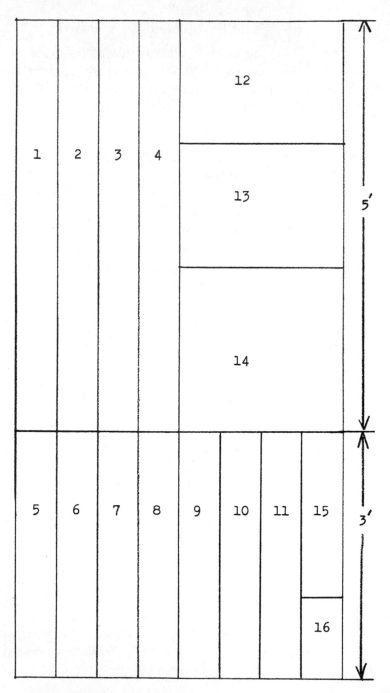

FIGURE 2: *Layout for cutting sheet of ¾-inch marine-grade fir plywood to make rack press.*

Marine-grade plywood should be used, because it is the only grade of plywood without voids and is also resistant to the inevitable moisture met with in wine pressing and cleanup operations. The frame of the press will have an open area twenty-four inches wide and thirty inches high. The polyethylene tray may be a "bus" tray found in restaurant supply stores, a pan sold for washing feet before entering a swimming pool, or another, similar pan of suitable size. If no suitable tray can be purchased, one can be made of wood that has been well paraffined to prevent leaking. The tray should have a hole bored in the bottom at one end to allow the wine to run out to another container. A rack is placed in the bottom of the tray, loosely woven cloth or plastic window screening is centered on the rack, pulp is piled in the center of the screen, and the four corners of the cloth are folded over the pulp. Another rack is placed on top of the cheese of pulp and the process repeated until three cheeses are in the press. Heavy blocks of wood are placed on the top rack and covered with a sheet of plastic. This latter prevents juice from squirting out as pressure is applied, but even more important, precludes the possibility of oil or hydraulic fluid dropping into the wine. The hydraulic jack, or equivalent heavy-duty screw jack, supplies pressure for extracting the liquid. Common automobile scissor jacks do not furnish enough pressure and are not strong enough to withstand the work load without bending out of shape. Racks for the press can be made of oak flooring fastened together with brass screws and painted with melted paraffin.

The most efficient way to press pulp is a stop-and-go technique of applying pressure until substantial resistance is met. At this point, application of pressure is stopped until the pomace runs dry, or between five and ten minutes. After this wait, additional pressure can be applied. When this process has been repeated two or three times, the press should be opened and the pulp stirred around. A second pressing cycle can then be initiated. Each load of pulp

Homemade rack press using steel channel beams. The plastic "bus" tray is supported by thick boards. Pressure is distributed evenly over the surface by the blocks under the hydraulic jack.

in the press should require between thirty and forty minutes if the suggested waiting intervals are observed. Application of continuous pressure without these interruptions may damage the press.

Mechanically adept home wine makers can make a juice extractor that is both gentle and thorough from an old spin-dry washing machine. In order to modify the machine for extracting juice, the basket should first be removed, and it and the tub examined for any chips or cracks in the enamel. The method for taking off the assembly that holds the agitator on Kenmore and Whirlpool machines is to heat it with a torch and prize it off as shown in the accompanying photograph. Directions for dismantling any particular brand of washing machine are found in repair manuals available at the local public library. Damaged enamel can be covered with epoxy paint to prevent exposure of the must or wine to bare metal.

When the crushed grapes are spun until all of the available liquid appears to have been removed, the basket should be stopped and the pomace redistributed. A five-minute draining period is then allowed, after which the spinning can be resumed to remove any remaining juice. The spinner will work satisfactorily for soft fruits and berries that cannot be successfully pressed in a conventional basket press. This is particularly true if a liner of loosely woven cloth is spread around the sides of the basket before the pomace is placed in the basket. While spinning may not remove quite as much liquid as pressing, the action is gentler and many of the cloudy or bitter materials that accompany pressed liquid are not extracted by the spinning action. This will give wines that clear more rapidly and mature sooner than when pressure is used.

Transferring large quantities of juice or wine from one container to another may be accomplished by pouring, siphoning, or pumping. Pouring wine from one container into another, except for decanting, usually creates too much aeration of the wine and is not recommended. Siphoning is a good way to transfer liquids, but it operates only when the receiving container is below the level of the liquid to be siphoned. Pumping aerates wine more than siphoning, but is more flexible and allows greater quantities to be moved in less time. Inexpensive pumps of the type used in photography, with housings and impellers made of inert plastics, are best for home wine makers. Without motors, these sell for as little as $8. A larger unit with motor included sells for approximately $38 and is good for many thousands of gallons.

The simplest and least expensive corker, described in our

Juice extractor improvised from basket-type washing machine.

list of basic equipment, leaves something to be desired in the way of efficiency when more than a few dozen bottles are to be corked. If the hypothetical goal of two hundred gallons is to be bottled, approximately a thousand bottles have to be located, cleaned, filled, corked, and stored. For this number of bottles an efficient bench or floor corker is a must. Hand-operated, lever-type corkers simply take too much effort for a task of such magnitude. In times past, a good deal of ingenuity was involved in the design of efficient hand corking devices, and if searched for with diligence, one of these may be found and purchased. Among currently available models, the Sanbri bench corker and some Italian floor models will meet the requirements for efficient performance. The best corkers compress the corks into a diameter that allows easy insertion into the bottle neck without excess strain on the cork by pinching or undue distortion.

Racks of various sizes and designs are available from sup-

Removing basket from washing machine. The retainer, which is force-fitted, is removed by heating and prying off.

A wine pump. Housing and impeller are made of non-contaminating plastic. This is useful in transferring large quantities of wine or must from one container to another.

ply houses, or they may be made to suit individual requirements. An efficient rack that consists of boards with alternating deep and shallow vees cut along one edge is shown on pages 85. These boards are mounted so they are spaced eight inches apart, with each shallow vee directly opposite a deep vee. Minimum space is needed for bottle storage, bottles are kept separate from each other, and any bottle can be removed without disturbing any other. If desired, several layers of bottles can be stored using the support of the vees, but of course individual removal of bottles is no longer possible. Other racks have been made of short lengths of clay or plastic pipe stacked so as to provide a separate receptacle for each bottle. These are attractive but require large amounts of space for the number of bottles stored. Square or diamond-shaped bins are also commonly employed, and when properly made are both efficient and attractive.

Where to locate these storage racks and the wine they hold is not as simple a problem as it once was, when most houses were built with cellars designed for storage of food and wine, with their cool darkness and freedom from vibration. Present-day basements usually include laundry, furnace, workshop, den, and other activities, and finding an area that is cool and

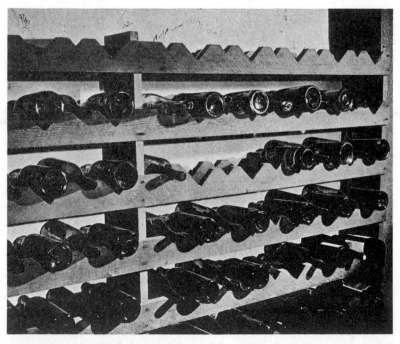

Simple but useful bottle-storage rack consisting of boards with alternate deep and shallow vees. This allows the bottles to be placed alternately front to back, saving space.

dark requires careful planning. A part of the room farthest from furnace and hot-water heater may be blocked off from the rest of the room by a frame of two-by-fours to which 1½-inch-thick sheets of polyurethane foam are attached. These sheets should extend from floor to ceiling, completely isolating the wine storage area from the rest of the cellar. If desired, a thermostat-controlled air conditioner can be installed to keep temperatures between 50° F and 60° F for optimum storage conditions.

Those who live in houses without basements have a more serious wine storage problem. In some of these houses there is enough room in the crawl space beneath the floor to store a considerable amount of wine. Access to the area is usually awkward, and in termite areas care must be taken to use nonedible storage racks. Apartment house dwellers, and those whose homes are built on concrete slabs, must settle for an inside closet away from heavily traveled areas, and outside walls with fluctuating temperatures. Such a closet, lined with polyurethane foam sheets and some provision for cooling, can keep wine quite well for long periods of time.

Ideally wine should be stored at from 50° F for white wines to about 55° F for red wines, and as mentioned earlier, in a dark, fairly humid place with minimum vibration. If these conditions are difficult to attain, wine can be stored in the coolest, most even temperature available. Wines stored at temperatures above optimum will mature earlier, but if temperatures are kept even, they will not be damaged. Needless to say, wine bottles should always be stored lying on their sides so corks are kept moist and do not shrink, thus preventing air from reaching and spoiling the vintage.

Because most homemade wines are unfiltered and will tend to throw a deposit as they age, bottles should be removed from storage to where they are to be consumed an hour or more before opening. They should be placed in an upright position so the deposit will drift to the bottom of the bottle. When the bottle is opened, it should be carefully decanted.

The correct way to decant wine is first to place a small funnel in the neck of the decanter. The bottle of wine is held close to the bottom, against a light that will show the deposit. The bottle is carefully and gradually tilted and the wine poured without gurgling until only a small amount of wine containing the deposit remains in the bottle. Careful decanting will leave a decanter full of clear wine, and an ounce or two of wine with dregs in the bottle. If the bottles are to be reused, they should be rinsed and allowed to drain before storing. Decanting avoids stirring the deposit, which can make the wine cloudy and sometimes bitter.

Decanting the wine. The light shining through the bottle allows any sediment to be seen and pouring stopped as it reaches the neck. The bottle should be held low enough to give a good view of the contents.

When decanting is complete, a small amount of wine and the dregs remain in the bottle, while the clear wine occupies the decanter.

Wine with heavy deposits that is intended to be used at some place other than where it has been stored can profitably be delivered a day or two before consumption, so it can be stood upright and the sediment allowed to settle before the wine is decanted and served. It is discouraging and unnecessary to have wines that have been made with care, stored patiently, and brought forward with pride, turn out to be cloudy and not bring credit to the producer. This situation can be avoided by delivering the wine a day or two before it is to be consumed.

5

Fruit Wines

This recipe for stone-fruit wines can be used for nectarines, peaches, apricots, plums, and cherries. The recipe will make five gallons of wine.

—For a dry table wine use 12–15 pounds of fruit and enough sugar to obtain a Balling reading of 22–24°.

—For a medium wine use 18–20 pounds of fruit and enough sugar for a Balling reading of 30–36°.

—Sweet wines should have 20–25 pounds of fruit and sufficient sugar added to have a Balling of 38–40°.

These ingredients will be necessary:

10–12 kernels from fruit pits
10 grams single-strength pectolytic enzyme
2 grams potassium metabisulfite
6 grams grape tannin
10 grams tartaric acid (citric acid may be used if preferred)
1 package Montrachet yeast
water to make five gallons.

Mash the fruit, allowing the stones to remain with the pulp. Remove 10–12 pits, and extract and crush kernels. Add crushed kernels to pulp in vat. Dissolve tannic acid, potassium metabisulfite, tartaric or citric acid, and pectolytic enzymes in a small amount of water, and add to the pulp. Add boiling water to make five gallons. Stir this mixture thoroughly and allow it to cool. When the temperature reaches 75° F, take a hydrometer reading, subtracting 1.5° Balling from the measurement to allow for solids other than sugar in the fresh must. For dry wine, measure out the sugar needed to obtain the desired Balling reading at the rate of ⅛ pound of sugar per degree per gallon. Withdraw one pint of fluid for each pound of sugar. Heat in a stainless-steel saucepan, dissolving the sugar, stirring well to make a clear syrup. Add syrup to contents of vat and stir well. For a medium wine, the total amount of sugar should be divided and added to the must in two equal portions, the second about three days after the first. For sweet wines, total sugar should be added in three equal portions, each about three days apart. In all cases, the first portion of the sugar syrup should be added to the wine immediately, while second and third additions of syrup should not take place unless the must is actively fermenting. If there are signs that fermentation is slowing down and becoming subdued, a check with the hydrometer is indicated to determine whether or not fermentation can be expected to handle the next addition of syrup without trouble.

Once the syrup is stirred into the must and the mixture allowed to cool to 70–75° F, a package of dry-wine yeast can be poured on one spot on top of the must. This will allow an active colony to develop before being dispersed throughout the must. The fermentation vat should then be covered and allowed to rest for eight to twelve hours. At the end of this time the must should be stirred thoroughly and a thermometer reading taken. If a liquid-yeast starter is used instead of the dry yeast, it too should be poured in one spot and allowed to multiply before being stirred into the must.

After stirring the must for the first time and reading the temperature, cover the fermentation vat once again and allow fermentation to continue. If the weather is moderate or cool, the must should be stirred once a day, following which thermometer and hydrometer readings are made and the results recorded in the fermentation log. A complete and permanent record of the progress of fermentation will provide valuable information in future wine making ventures. If the thermometer rises above 75–78° F, the must should be cooled, and if it falls below about 50°, warming may keep fermentation from sticking. If two or three days pass with no change in the hydrometer reading, it should be assumed that fermentation has stuck.

Stuck fermentations usually result from one or more of the following conditions:

a. The must has grown too warm for the yeast, which is losing its virility and dying. In this case the best action is to prevent must temperatures from exceeding the recommended maximum of 78°. Cooling the must is the best remedy, while aeration by vigorous stirring or withdrawing a portion of the must and pouring it from a height of about four feet back into the vat helps to restore yeast activity. As a last resort it may become necessary to reinoculate the must with fresh yeast.

b. Too much sugar was added at one time, making a concentrated syrup in which yeasts are incapable of functioning. In this case some of the syrup may be removed, and water that has been boiled and allowed to cool may be added to reduce the hydrometer reading to below 30° Balling. If indicated a large part of the heavy syrup can be removed and gradually added again to actively fermenting must that has less sugar. Such additions should be in small enough doses so that yeast activity is not reduced. Reinoculation with fresh yeast may also be necessary.

c. The must has become colder than the yeast can tolerate. This form of stuck fermentation usually occurs during a sudden cold snap. Heating the must and aeration usually overcome the problem. When must temperature is slowly reduced over a period of time, yeasts can remain active to quite low temperatures, especially if fermentation has been allowed to become quite vigorous before temperatures are lowered. There are also some special "cold fermenting" yeasts that over generations have been acclimated to low temperatures and retain vigor down to 40° F.

When the hydrometer shows a Balling reading of between 4° and 6°, the new wine should be drained off and the pulp placed in a pressing bag and squeezed to remove as much of the liquid as possible. Both free-run and pressed liquid should be combined and siphoned into a clean five-gallon jug. The jug should be filled to within one to one and a half inches of the brim. Any drops of wine left on the neck should be wiped away with a fresh paper towel and a fermentation lock inserted, or the neck should be covered with a sheet of plastic film secured by a rubber band. Place the jug in a cool (60–65°) location where the temperature will remain quite constant and little vibration will be encountered. In about thirty days, or when the lees, or sediment, are deposited to a depth of about one-half or three-fourths inch in thickness, place a block of two-by-four wood under one side of the jug so that it will tilt. The following day, rack the clear wine off the lees.

Place the opening of the siphon tube a few inches below the top of the wine, start the siphon action, and gradually move the tube down until the opening is about an inch above the lees. The outlet of the siphon should be near the top of the receiving jug to allow the wine to flow down the inside walls in a wide, shallow stream. This aerates the wine, helping secondary fermentation. If the hydrometer reading taken at this time shows zero Balling or slightly higher, fermentation is not complete. When the wine is completely fermented, the hydrometer reading will be about −1.5° Balling.

When the clear wine is racked, fill the new jug once again to within one to one and a half inches of the brim with the same kind of wine, if available, or with cool boiled water, and add 1 gram of potassium metabisulfite dissolved in a little of the wine. Wipe the neck dry and place a new cover of plastic film over the top of the jug, return it to its cool location, allow it to remain another ninety days or so.

At the end of this time, rack the wine again, but for this

and subsequent rackings place the outlet of the tube at the bottom of the receiving jug so the wine will be exposed to the least amount of air. The only time wine should be aerated after the first racking is when it has developed the smell of hydrogen sulfide (rotten eggs), when aeration and addition of potassium metabisulfite are indicated remedies. Fill the jug completely as before and reseal with new plastic film. If more deposits appear, the wine should be racked as needed to remove them. Lees should not be allowed to remain in the wine too long, since they may be partially hydrolized and develop unwanted flavors in the wine.

If oak flavor is considered an improvement, boiled sterile oak chips may be added at the time of the second racking. These chips will also help to settle any haze that develops in the wine. Oak flavor may become too pronounced if the chips remain in the wine for too long a time. Tasting at intervals will allow the wine maker to judge when the chips should be removed.

When all fermentation has stopped and the wine is brilliantly clear, it may be bottled.

Pome fruits, such as apples, pears, or quinces, usually have firmer flesh than do stone fruits and must be ground or chopped before fermentation. This may be done with knives, food grinder, or specially constructed apple grinders that look like the familiar grape crusher but are made with sets of grinding teeth in flywheel-controlled rollers.

This recipe for pome fruit will make five gallons of light dry table wine:

> 15–20 pounds of fruit, crushed
> sugar to bring five gallons of must to 22–24° Balling
> 10 grams pectolytic enzyme
> 2 grams potassium metabisulfite
> 10 grams malic or citric acid (5 grams for cider apples)
> 5 grams tannin (necessary only for apples)
> 1 packet Montrachet yeast
> water to make up five gallons.

Grind the fruit to a pulp, allowing it to drop into a vat containing a solution of one gram of potassium metabisulfite in one gallon of water. This solution acts as an anti-oxidant and will keep the fruit and juice from becoming brown. After the fruit has been pulped, add the remaining potassium metabisulfite, the acid, the tannin dissolved in a little water, and the pectolytic enzyme. Pour boiling water to make up five gallons over the mixture and allow it to cool. When the must reaches 70° F, take a hydrometer reading and add sugar at the rate of ⅛ pound per gallon of must per degree Balling desired, to obtain a total Balling reading of 22–24°. With-

Cider making on a farm in Normandy, from Diderot's Encyclopedia of Sciences, Arts, and Trades. *The apples are sorted into the pie-shaped container, then crushed by the stone wheel running in the peripheral trough. Crushed pulp is then transferred to the Roman-style press, where turning of the screw forces the other end of the massive beam against the container with the pulp. Such presses were used for pressing grapes until comparatively recent times.*

draw liquid sufficient to make syrup, dissolve sugar in it, and return it to vat, stirring thoroughly. When the must cools to 70°, add the yeast all in one place. Cover the vat and set it aside for twelve hours. At the end of this time, stir the must to disperse yeast and add a bit of oxygen. Stirring also mixes pulp and liquid and equalizes temperature in the must. Read temperature and hydrometer, entering figures in log. Several days later, when hydrometer reads about 4° Balling, dip out must, pouring into pressing bag. Siphon remaining liquid into 5-gallon jug, adding wine expressed from pulp. Top off the jug, seal, and allow to settle thirty days. Rack into fresh jug, reseal, and allow to rest another sixty to ninety days. After this, other rackings can take place as needed.

Apple wine should have one gram of potassium metabisulfite added at each racking. When the wine is brilliantly clear and fermentation completed, bottle and store.

From *The Housekeeper's Receipt Book, or The Repository of Domestic Knowledge,* published in London in 1813, we give this recipe for quince wine:

"Gather twenty large quinces dry and ripe, wipe them with a cloth and grate them so as not to touch the core. Put the quince into a gallon of boiling water and let it boil gently a quarter of an hour: strain it into a pan on two pounds of refined sugar, put in the peels of two lemons, and squeeze the juice through a sieve. Stir it about till it is cool, put in a toast of bread with a little yeast on it, and let it stand close covered till the next day. Take out the toast and lemon, keep it three months and bottle it off."

This recipe can be adapted, almost without change, to make wine in the manner recommended in this book. The modifications would be to let the boiled, strained juice cool, then take a hydrometer reading, add sugar needed to reach 24° Balling. Forget the toast and simply add a package of Montrachet yeast. After the lemon is removed, the wine should be allowed to undergo secondary fermentation in a jug filled to within an inch of the brim and sealed with a fermentation lock or plastic film.

A delicious wine can be made from pomegranates if the uncrushed fruit is pressed. If the fruit is ground or crushed before pressing, the bitter substances in the skin and seeds predominate in the wine and make it unpalatable. The only other possibility is the tedious chore of peeling the fruit and removing the hundreds of tiny fruit-coated seeds, and pressing these. Pressing the whole fruit is the only practical way to approach the problem, and unless a heavy-duty rack press with hydraulic pressure is available, this wine should not be attempted. Enough tannin will be extracted during the pressing to eliminate the need for adding any of this material.

To make five gallons of pomegranate wine use:

> 20 pounds of pomegranates
> water to make five gallons
> 2 grams potassium metabisulfite
> 5 grams citric acid
> sugar to obtain a hydrometer reading of 22–26° Balling
> 1 package Montrachet yeast.

Press the pomegranates, extracting juice. Add sufficient water to make up five gallons. Add potassium metabisulfite and citric acid. Test for sugar content. Remove one pint of juice/water mixture for each pound of sugar required to obtain desired Balling reading. Heat liquid and dissolve sugar to make a syrup. Add syrup to vat containing pressed juice and water. When mixture has cooled to 70° F, add yeast, pouring in one location on surface of liquid. Cover, and allow to remain twelve hours. At that time stir thoroughly, take temperature reading, record, and re-cover the must, allowing it to sit for another twenty-four hours. Stir, and check and record temperature and hydrometer readings on a daily basis until the hydrometer reads about 2° Balling. When the hydrometer reaches the 2° point, allow the must to stand quietly for twenty-four hours after it has last been stirred, then rack as much of the clear liquid as possible from the vat into a clean five-gallon jug. Top off the five-gallon jug with a similar wine or water that has been boiled and allowed to cool, seal with plastic film, and allow to stand in an even temperature for thirty days. At that time, rack into another five-gallon jug, top off, seal, and set aside for another sixty to ninety days, when a second racking should be made. Rack and store as necessary to obtain a perfectly clear wine, then bottle. The wine will be pleasant after a year, delightful the second year, and superb after the third year.

Figs have no discernible acid, so for a well-balanced wine citric or tartaric acid should be added to raise total acidity to about six grams per gallon. Fig wine is best made into a medium or a sweet wine, rather than a dry wine; therefore total acid will be less than with most dry wines. The addition of tannin will also help reduce the natural blandness of the wine and give it more character.

Figs have very tender skins, which are easily abraded or split, and should be selected with caution to avoid any openings that can expose the fruit to acetobacterial infection. To make five gallons of medium fig wine use:

> 20 pounds of figs (blue or white)
> water to make 5 gallons
> sugar to obtain Balling reading of 32–34°
> 2.5 grams potassium metabisulfite
> 10 grams citric or tartaric acid
> 5 grams tannin
> 1 package Montrachet yeast.

Mash figs with wood pestle. Pour boiling water to make five gallons over figs. When cool, test with hydrometer for Balling reading. Withdraw approximately half a gallon of liquid. Add sugar necessary to give total Balling reading of

32–34°. Heat and stir to make syrup. Add acids and potassium metabisulfite to must. Pour in syrup, stirring until completely mixed, cover, and allow to stand twelve hours. Pour in contents of 1 package of Montrachet yeast—all in one place. Cover, and twelve hours later stir and take thermometer and hydrometer readings. Repeat every twenty-four hours until hydrometer reading is reduced to 6° Balling. Strain pulp through jelly bag, and press. Place 2 grams potassium metabisulfite in 5-gallon jug. Pour free-run and pressed wine into jug, swirling wine around in partially filled jug to dissolve potassium metabisulfite. Fill jug to within one inch of brim, adding cool boiled water if necessary. Wipe neck of jug clean with paper towel and cover with plastic film held down by rubber band.

It is best to have experience with other wines and learn the fundamentals of testing for acid and sulfur dioxide content before making fig wine. Fig wine has few of the natural buffers that wines made from high-acid fruit contain, and for that reason is quite tricky, with a good chance of turning out to be an elegant fig vinegar.

Pineapple makes a pleasant dry white wine with an exotic, tantalizing flavor when made according to this recipe. Pineapples should be selected that are free from bruises and over-ripe areas. If the spear-shaped leaves can be easily plucked from the crown of the fruit, the pineapple is ripe enough to be used for wine. If the leaf resists removal in more than the slightest degree, the fruit is not ready and should be passed over. For five gallons of dry table wine the following will be required:

15 pounds of pineapple
water to make five gallons
2 grams potassium metabisulfite
5 grams tannin dissolved in water
sugar to obtain a hydrometer reading of 24° Balling
1 package Montrachet yeast.

Remove about a half inch from the top and the bottom of the pineapple, quarter the remainder, and chop fine without peeling. Pour boiling water to make five gallons over the fruit. When somewhat cool, add potassium metabisulfite and tannin. Pectolytic enzymes are not required for pineapple, because they appear naturally in the fruit. When the temperature reaches 70° F, stir well and take a hydrometer reading. Withdraw one half gallon of the liquid and add sugar to obtain 24° Balling. Add syrup to vat, stirring until completely mixed. Cover and cool to 70° F again. Add yeast and allow to stand twelve hours. At the end of that time stir thoroughly, re-cover, and allow to ferment for twenty-four hours. Stir and take thermometer and hydrometer readings daily and record progress, until hydrometer reads 4° Balling. Remove pulp and press dry, pouring all liquid into 5-gallon jug. Top off, seal, and allow secondary fermentation to take place. Rack in thirty, ninety, and 120 days. When sparkling clear and all fermentation is completed, bottle and store for one year.

Although for most culinary purposes tomatoes are treated as vegetables, in wine making they are processed in much the same way as other fruit. For convenience they will be included in that category. Tomatoes make a light, tawny-colored wine that provides an unusual and pleasant accompaniment to salad (with minimum vinegar), *pasta*, and fish dishes. It must be allowed to age for two years before being drunk, and can be unpleasant, just as can Cabernet Sauvignon, when consumed before it is ready. To make five gallons of tomato wine the following ingredients will be required. This will make a dry table wine.

    20 pounds vine-ripened tomatoes
    2 grams potassium metabisulfite
    2 grams table salt
    water to make five gallons
    sugar to obtain Balling reading of 24°
    1 package Montrachet yeast.

Every effort should be made to obtain home-grown, vine-ripened tomatoes. Store-bought tomatoes are grown for their ability to withstand shipping and rough handling, rather than their flavor, and are picked green so that they will ripen after they reach the market. Both these features effectively reduce chances of obtaining really flavorful fruit from such sources, and the ultimate quality of the wine will suffer.

Place whole, vine-ripe, unbruised tomatoes in fermentation vat, sprinkle with potassium metabisulfite, and pour two gallons of boiling water over them. After five minutes, mash the tomatoes with a pestle. Add sufficient boiling water to make up five gallons. When liquid is cool, test with hydrometer. Add sufficient sugar to result in hydrometer reading of 24° Balling. Stir thoroughly to dissolve all sugar. Add salt and yeast. Cover and allow to stand overnight. Stir well the following day, and cover again. Stir and take temperature and hydrometer readings daily. When hydrometer reaches 4–6° Balling, strain out pulp, placing in jelly bag, and squeeze as dry as possible. Transfer liquid to 5-gallon jug, filling to within one inch of brim. Cover with plastic film. Allow to remain about thirty days, then rack. Rack again sixty days later, then as necessary if sediment in jug reaches a quarter inch in thickness. When fermentation has finished and wine is perfectly clear, bottle. Do not serve until wine has matured two years. The wine may be tasted from time to time to see how it is developing, but it should not be offered to guests until it has aged for the recommended two years.

In *Dr. Chase's Recipes; or, Information for Everybody: An Invaluable Collection of About 800 Practical Recipes*, published by the author, 1867, the following method of making tomato wine appears:

> "Express the juice from clean ripe tomatoes, and to each gallon of it (without any water), put brown sugar, 4 pounds.
>
> "Put in the sugar immediately, or before fermentation

begins. This ought to be done in making any fruit wine. Something of the character of a cheese press, hoop and cloth is the best plan to squeeze out the juice of tomatoes or other fruits. Let the wine stand in a keg or barrel for two or three months, then draw off into bottles, carefully avoiding the sediment. It makes a most delightful wine having all the beauties of flavor belonging to the tomato, and I have no doubt all its medical properties also, either as a tonic in disease, or as a beverage for those who are in the habit of using intoxicating beverages, and if such persons would have the good sense to make some wine of this kind, and use it instead of rot-gut whisky, there would not be one-hundredth part of the 'snake-in-the-boot' that now curses our land."

Citrus wines are best made by extracting the juice with a juicer and grating a portion of the colored part of the rind into the liquid. Any of the meaty part of the fruit can remain in the must, but care should be exercised to eliminate any part of the white, pulpy inner rind. This part of the fruit will make wine very bitter. The grated "zest" of the skin also contains strong oils, so that only a portion, say 20 per cent, of the fruit should be grated for zest. This portion can be even smaller for wine made from lemons or grapefruit. For a dry citrus wine, the following proportions are suggested:

12–15 pounds of fruit
2 grams potassium metabisulfite
10 grams pectolytic enzyme
water to make five gallons
sugar to obtain hydrometer reading of 24° Balling
1 package Montrachet yeast.

Place whole fruit in large container. Pour boiling water over fruit, allowing it to stand until cool enough to handle with comfort. Grate rinds of about 20 per cent of fruit, placing zest in fermentation vat. Halve remaining fruit and squeeze juice into vat. Add potassium metabisulfite, pectolytic enzyme, and water to make five gallons. Take hydrometer reading. Withdraw a half to one gallon of liquid, and heat, dissolving sugar needed to raise Balling reading to 24–26°. Return to fermentation vat, stirring well into the rest of the juice. When must reaches 70° F, add yeast, cover, and allow to ferment for twenty-four hours. Stir and take temperature and hydrometer readings daily. When hydrometer reaches 2–4° Balling, strain out pulp and transfer liquid to 5-gallon jug. Fill to within one inch of brim and cover with plastic film held down by rubber band. Allow to continue fermentation for thirty days, then rack clear fluid from sediment. Fill new container to within one inch of brim, reseal, and allow to rest another thirty to sixty days. When sediment is reduced to a thin film on the bottom of the jug after a thirty-day wait, the wine is clear, and fermentation has stopped, then it may be bottled. These wines will require various intervals to mature, orange and tangerine needing the least amount, while grapefruit will require the longest time to lose its astringency and become pleasurable to drink.

Lemon, lime, and probably grapefruit wines will all benefit from use as summer drinks, diluted with sparkling water or other carbonated beverage for greatest satisfaction. Orange and tangerine can be consumed without dilution, but even these make great coolers.

The following recipe for orange wine comes from the book called *Open Air Grape Culture, a Practical Treatise on Garden and Vineyard Culture of the Vine, and the Manufacture of Domestic Wine*, by John Phin, published in New York in 1863:

"Seville Oranges are used for this purpose; they are best in March. For 18 gallons of wine, half a chest of oranges are required. Pare the rinds from about a dozen or two dozen, as more or less of the bitter will be agreeable. Pour over this a quart or two of boiling water, and after letting this stand for twelve hours, strain off the water, which extracted much of the essential of the oranges. Take the peel off entirely from the remainder of the oranges, squeeze the juice through a bag or sieve, and put into a cask with about forty-five pounds of white sugar. Soak the pulp in water for 24 hours, and after straining this, add it to the cask. Repeat this several times till the cask is full. Stir the whole well with a stick until the sugar is dissolved, then set it to ferment. The fermentation is slower than with currant wine, but may be heard hissing for several weeks, when this subsides, close the bung hole. The wine requires to be kept in the cask a year before it is bottled."

Prunes and raisins, and apricots, dates, apples, pears, etc. when dried, contain the essence of flavor and sugar with a minimum of moisture. Consequently, less dried fruit than fresh fruit is needed for wine. The concentrated, sun-enriched flavor also tends to make a richer-tasting wine, more suitable to a medium or a sweet wine than the dry type. In selecting dried fruit for wine making, it is best to try to obtain unsulfured fruit. Sulfur dioxide will be added to the must during the wine making process, and if the fruit itself has a sufficient amount it will be difficult to ferment and may end up with a distinct flavor of sulfur. For five gallons of medium wine the following ingredients will be required:

8–10 pounds of dried, pitted fruit
10 grams citric acid, or juice and zest of 5 lemons
4 grams grape tannin (omit from raisin wine)
2 grams potassium metabisulfite
water to make five gallons
Sugar to obtain hydrometer reading of 32–36° Balling
1 package Montrachet yeast.

Chop the pitted fruit into small pieces. If a knife is being used for this task, be sure it is a French chef's knife and that it is correctly used. If so, the task can be much more pleasant and efficient than if other kinds of knives are employed. When the knife edge becomes sticky from the fruit, the job can be made easier by dipping the edge in a mound of powdered sugar to coat it and reduce the amount of fruit that clings to the knife. Scissors can also be used, as can a meat grinder with very coarse blades. When the fruit is chopped, sprinkle citric acid or lemon juice, zest, grape tannin, and potassium metabisulfite over fruit. Take half of the water, bring to a boil, and pour over all ingredients in fermenting vat. Cover and allow to stand twenty-four hours. Stir very thoroughly, and when liquid has come to rest, pour yeast on surface. Cover and allow to ferment for twelve hours. Uncover and stir, taking thermometer and hydrometer measurements. Repeat daily until hydrometer reads 8–10° Balling. Remove pulp into jelly bag and siphon remaining liquid into 5-gallon jug. Press pomace in jelly bag and add extruded liquid to 5-gallon jug. Add remaining water, filling to within 1–1½ inches of brim. Seal with plastic film and set aside in cool place. Rack at intervals of thirty, ninety, and 120 days. When wine is clear and fermentation completed, bottle, and store until mature.

Various combinations of dried fruit or dried and fresh fruit and flowers can be made using the basic recipe given above. It should be remembered that if a light, dry table wine is desired the proportion of fresh material to dried should be about two to one, with a general maximum of three pounds of material for each gallon of wine desired. A traditional recipe for a combination fruit wine is given below.

This recipe, for elder/raisin wine, is from *The Experienced English Housekeeper*, a household recipe book that first appeared in 1769 and went through at least eleven editions. Elizabeth Raffald, the author, must have been an exceedingly busy person, because in addition to writing the cookbook, Mrs. Raffald was married in 1763, and had first a shop and then three inns in succession. She had sixteen daughters in eighteen years, and died in 1781.

"To every gallon of water put 6 pounds of Malaga raisins shred small, put them into a vessel, pour water on them boiling hot, and let it stand 9 days, stirring it thrice every day, get the elderberries when full ripe, pick them off the stalks, put them into an earthen pot, and set them in a moderate oven all night, then strain them through a coarse cloth, and to every gallon of liquor add one quart of this juice, stir it well together, then toast a slice of bread and spread three spoonfuls of yest [sic] on both sides and put them in your wine, and let it work a day or two, then turn it into your cask, fill it up as it works over, when it has done working, close it up and let it stand one year."

This recipe, with a few simple changes, can be used today. Dry wine yeast should be substituted for the toast with "yest" smeared on both sides. The wine should be allowed to work (ferment) until it reaches about 6° Balling, and when it is put into a cask (or better yet, 5-gallon jugs), it should be beyond the stage of active fermentation, in which it would "work over."

6

Wines from Flowers, Herbs, Berries, Teas, Honey, Preserves, and Concentrates

The following recipe will make five gallons of a moderately dry wine from carnations, orange or lemon blossoms, marigolds, roses, daisies, dandelions, elder flowers, goldenrod, violets, etc. Because of the very small amount of natural sugar contained in most flowers, a specific amount of sugar is given in this recipe.

4–5 gallons of flower petals, loosely packed
4½ gallons water
15 pounds sugar
10 grams grape tannin
50 grams tartaric or citric acid
5 grams potassium metabisulfite
20 grams yeast nutrient or 2 pounds chopped raisins
1 package Montrachet yeast.

Flower petals with no green parts attached should be picked when dry and placed in the fermenting vat; two gallons of boiling water should then be poured over them. They should macerate from twelve to thirty hours depending on the strength of their fragrance and of the flavor desired in the wine. Elder-flower wine needs only 1½ gallons of flowers. These are shaken off the stems and macerated a maximum of eight hours. Do not use more than the recommended 1½ gallons of blossoms, and do not macerate longer than eight hours, or the resulting wine will be unpleasantly strong in flavor. After pouring the boiling water over the flower petals, cover the fermentation vat with a cloth or a sheet of polyethylene. Stir the mixture every eight hours. At the end of the maceration period strain out the flower petals into a pressing bag and press them dry. Dissolve the sugar, tannin, tartaric acid, potassium metabisulfite, and yeast nutrient in the remaining 2½ gallons of water and heat until the mixture is clear and all solids dissolved. Pour the heated syrup into the fermentation vat. Mix thoroughly. When it has cooled to 70° F, add the yeast in one place, sprinkling it in an area about four inches in diameter. Cover the fermentation vat with a cloth or a plastic sheet. After eight hours stir thoroughly and take temperature and hydrometer measurements. Repeat stirring and measurement every twelve hours until hydrometer shows zero on the Balling scale. Transfer to 5-gallon jug to continue secondary fermentation. Fill jug to within one inch of brim, cover with plastic film, and fasten down with rubber bands. Rack in thirty, ninety, and 120 days. Flower wines should clear rapidly, but will improve with age.

Here is another recipe for elder-flower wine, this time from *Jennie June's American Cookery Book*, by Mrs. J. C. Croly, published in 1878:

"Allow a gallon of water, and three pounds of sugar to every quart of blossoms stripped from the stalks, boil and skim the sugar and water, and pour it over the flowers boiling hot. To every gallon of the liquor add a small table spoon of home-brewed hop yeast, and the juice of a lemon; stir thoroughly together. Let the whole ferment for three days in an open vessel of wood or earthen, the top entirely covered with a thick woolen blanket. At the end of three days, strain it through a sieve, and whisk the white of an egg, beaten to a froth, through the wine. Put at the bottom of the cask chopped raisins, in the proportion of three or four pounds to every six gallons of wine, pour in the wine and close the bung. In six months it will be fit to bottle."

This results in a very interesting, full-bodied, flavorful wine. The recipe is excellent in all respects, with the possible exception of closing the bung after adding the wine to the raisins. A water seal would be indicated to let off any carbon dioxide that might accumulate. Another precautionary step would be to top off the cask at least every other week to prevent the wine from turning to vinegar.

Herbs have been intimately associated with wine ever since the earliest wine maker tried to cover up the taste of souring wine with plants that would disguise the unpleasant flavor. All the herbs listed in the Appendix under their common and Latin names have been at one time or another employed in the flavoring of wines or cordials.

Cato the Censor, in his book *De Agri Cultura*, written in the second century B.C., gives this recipe for wine flavored with juniper, which he says is good for lumbago:

"Take juniper wood from a tree 5 inches thick and chop it to small pieces. Boil the wood in 7 quarts of old wine. When cool, strain the wine and store it. Take a tablespoon each morning before breakfast."

Cato provides another herb-wine recipe, this one made from bay leaves, and since the dried bay leaves are fermented with the must, it is more truly a wine than the concoction of juniper wood boiled in wine.

"Dry bay leaves (or black myrtle) in the shade until vintage time. Take 1 gallon of the bay leaves and grind them, put them into 3.6 gallons of fresh grape must. Seal and allow to ferment. When fermentation has stopped, rack the wine off the ground-up bay leaves. This wine is good for colic, pain in the side and indigestion."

Almost 2,000 years after Cato we find the following recipe for an herb wine called "English Sack" in a formulary called

The Compleat Housewife, by E. Smith. This is from the fifteenth edition, published in 1753:

> "To every quart of water put a sprig of rue, and to every gallon a handful of fennel roots. Boil these half an hour, then strain it out and to every gallon of this liquor put three pounds of honey, boil it two hours and skim it well; when it is cold, pour it off, and turn it into the vessel, or such cask as is fit for it. Keep it a year in the vessel, and then bottle it; it is very good sack."

That recipe, and others like it found in the household guides and cookbooks of the day, might very well provide a partial answer to a puzzle that has intrigued wine historians: what is sack? The name became very popular in the late-sixteenth and seventeenth centuries describing a wine imported from Italy, Spain, and other south European countries in large quantities. No adequate description of how it was made or what ingredients it contained or why it disappeared from commerce has yet been found. It appears to have been a robust wine, possibly fortified, presumably having added herbs, that was gradually replaced by sherry as we now know it.

Many so-called herb wines are infusions made by soaking the leaves, flowers, or roots of herbs in wine or spirits. These can generally be made by chopping or grinding the part of the plant to be used, macerating for anywhere from a few hours to several months in wine or spirits, and serving as desired.

Other variations rely upon distillation of a wine made from flowers or herbs. A typical recipe of this sort is that given by Sir Hugh Plat, who graduated from St. John's College, Cambridge, in 1571, and was the author of several household recipe and cookbooks. This is from his *Delights for Ladies,* published in London in 1609.

> *"How to Draw the True Spirit of Roses,*
> *and So of All Other Herbs and Flowers*

"Macerate the rose in his owne juice, adding thereunto, being temperately warm, a convenient portion either of yeast or ferment. Leaue thē a few daies in fermentation, till they have gotten a strong and heady smell, beginning to incline towards vinegar, then distil them in balneo [water bath] in glass bodies luted to their helms (happely a limbecke will do better and rid faster) and draw so long as you find any scent of the Rose to come, then redistil or rectify the same so often till you have purchased a perfect spirit of the Rose. You may also ferment the iuice of Roses onlie, and after distil the same."

"Luting" usually consists of filling the cracks or spaces between various parts of the still, usually with a paste made of flour and water. A "limbecke" is an alembic, or retort, commonly used for distilling over a direct fire rather than the balneo, or water bath, called for by Sir Hugh.

Herb wines can have the exact amount of sugar specified, since they, like flowers, have primarily flavoring and medicinal qualities to add to the wine, but contribute no sugar. Where raisins are employed to supply yeast nutrients, their sugar should be measured after they have been chopped and macerated for twenty-four hours. At that time the hydrometer should be used to measure the sugar contributed by the raisins, and the balance desired added in the form of granulated sugar.

This recipe will make five gallons of a medium-dry wine:

10 ounces of spices or dry herbs (or about 4 pounds of fresh herbs)
4½ gallons water
15½ pounds sugar
25 grams tartaric acid
15 grams yeast nutrient or 2 to 3 pounds raisins (chopped)
1 package of Montrachet yeast.

Macerate the herbs by placing them in the fermenting vat and pouring two gallons of boiling water over them. Allow to remain for an average of forty-eight hours, then bring the remaining two and a half gallons of water to a boil, dissolve the sugar in it, and pour into the vat. Add the tartaric acid and the yeast nutrient or chopped raisins and allow to cool to about 70° F. When the solution has reached that temperature, yeast should be added and the solution allowed to ferment for about twelve hours before being stirred. The must should be stirred daily thereafter, following which, temperature and hydrometer measurements are to be taken. This process should continue until the initial fermentation is complete and the hydrometer reads zero Balling. At that time the liquid should be strained off the herbs and racked into a 5-gallon jug. If any space remains in the bottle, it should be filled with cold boiled water. Rack as necessary, and bottle when clear and still.

It might be interesting to quote a recipe for an herb wine that was given to Samuel Pepys by Dr. Burnett in order to clear up an ulcer that was bothering the diarist:

"Take of yᵉ Rootes of Marsh-Mallows foure ounces, of Cumfry, of Liquorish, of each two ounces, of yᵉ fflowers of Sᵗ· John's Wort two handsfull, of yᵉ Leaves of Plantan, of Alehoofe, of each three handfulls, of Selfheal, of Red Roses, of each one Handfull, of Cynament, of Nutmeg, of each half an ounce. Beate them well, then powre upon them one quart of old Rhenish wine, and about six houres after strayne it and clarify it with yᵉ white of an Egge, and with a sufficient quantity of sugar, boyle it to yᵉ consistence of a Syrrup and reserve it for use.

"Dissolve one spoonfull of this Syrrup in every draught of ale or beere you drink. Morning and evening swallow yᵉ quantity of an hazle-nutt of Cyprus Terebintine. . . . Old Canary or Malaga wine you may drinke to three or 4 glasses, but noe new wine, and what wine you drinke, lett it bee at meales."

Most berries have a similar balance of sugar and acid,

though of course quite different flavors. For that reason they can, for the most part, be treated in a similar manner. Berries can be used for dry, medium, or sweet wines, as the wine maker chooses. The following recipe will make five gallons of dry wine from blackberries, strawberries, huckleberries, raspberries, blueberries, or any of the hybrids such as loganberries or boysenberries.

> 13 pounds of berries
> 10 grams pectolytic enzyme
> 3 grams potassium metabisulfite
> 4 gallons of water
> sugar to reach a hydrometer reading of 24° Balling
> 1 package Montrachet yeast.

If the berries have grown near a dusty road, or if they are store-bought, they should be washed in running water for at least fifteen minutes. A good way to do this without damaging the berries and losing valuable juice is to pour them carefully into a container half full of water, then run a hose into the container, allowing water to run over the edges. The berries can be kept in the container by tying a piece of netting or cheesecloth over the top of the container and running the water through this. Water can then easily be drained off the berries by tilting the container. Place the cleaned berries in the fermentation vat, add pectolytic enzyme and potassium metabisulfite, and crush the berries with a pestle, stirring so all of the berries are mashed. Pour the entire amount of boiling water over the fruit, cover, and allow to cool. When cool, check with hydrometer to determine how much sugar to add. Withdraw about one gallon of juice and heat sufficiently to dissolve sugar. Pour this syrup into vat, stirring well, then check temperature. If it is not higher than 75° F, yeast may be added and the vat covered and allowed to stand for twenty-four hours. Stir and take thermometer and hydrometer readings daily. When hydrometer reaches 4–6° Balling, strain out pulp and squeeze dry in a pressing bag. Siphon liquid into 5-gallon jug, filling to within one inch of top, and seal. Rack when sediment reaches a half to three-quarters inch in depth. Bottle when completely clear and still. Most berry wines clear rapidly and can usually be consumed early. Nevertheless it is advised that half of the vintage be set aside and not touched until at least a year old; it will have improved in the interim.

Berry wines that should be treated differently are elderberry, gooseberry, and cranberry. Each of these is discussed individually.

The mention of elderberry wine almost automatically brings to mind the picture of Lavender and Old Lace ladies primly serving elderberry wine and cakes in a room full of antiques. Unfortunately, unless properly made and aged, elderberry wine can taste very much like Arsenic and Old Lace—combined!

Properly made and fully aged, elderberry can be an excellent dry, medium, or even sweet wine. In fact, elderberries became an important part of the manufacture of port—so much so that in efforts to regulate the production of that wine, laws were passed in Portugal in 1756 that required destruction of all elder bushes throughout the Douro Valley and all other port-wine regions.

Elderberry wine should never be made by fermenting the whole berries. This method will extract so much tannin that the wine will not be palatable for six or seven years. The following recipe will make five gallons of robust dry elderberry wine:

    10 pounds of elderberries
    10 grams tartaric or citric acid
    3 grams potassium metabisulfite
    2 gallons of water
    additional water to make five gallons
    sugar to obtain hydrometer reading of 24° Balling
    1 package Montrachet yeast.

When picking elderberries, care should be taken to remove all but the tiny thin parts of the stems. Any coarse, thick stems should be removed, and preferably all stems should be eliminated. Most berries will have an accumulation of dust and should be washed in the manner described for berry wines.

Pour the washed berries into a container other than the fermentation vat, and add acid and potassium metabisulfite. Crush them thoroughly with a pestle, and pour the two gallons of boiling water over the fruit. When cool, strain and press the berries through a pressing bag. Pour the liquid into the fermentation vat and add sufficient water to make five gallons. Take a hydrometer reading, withdraw one gallon of liquid, heat, and add sugar, stirring until completely dissolved. Pour into fermentation vat and mix well with remaining liquid. When temperature reaches 70° F, add yeast. Cover; stir and test each day until hydrometer reads zero Balling. Rack into 5-gallon jug, filling to within one inch of brim, seal, and allow to undergo secondary fermentation. Rack as indicated by the deposit of sediment, and bottle when entirely clear and still.

Elderberries lend themselves to combination with ginger and raisins (see Mrs. Raffald's recipe) and other dried fruit. They also have enough substance to make excellent medium and sweet wines.

Gooseberries are a problem! Some varieties make excellent wine, while others are simply too acid, and even if heavily sweetened make wines that are unpleasantly sour. They are also fiendish to pick, as anyone who has tried to extract an elusive berry deep in a bush can testify.

If the "Poorman" variety is available, the intrepid wine maker who wants to try his hand at gooseberry wine stands the best chance of making a finished product of good flavor and body. Home-grown gooseberries have one advantage for wine makers. They usually ripen all at one time, so the entire bush can be stripped. Five gallons of a medium-dry wine can be made with this recipe:

15 pounds of ripe gooseberries (discard any that are damaged or moldy)
10 grams pectolytic enzyme
3 grams potassium metabisulfite
water to make five gallons
sugar to obtain hydrometer reading of 32° Balling
1 bottle Madeira, Tokay, or Malaga yeast.

If gooseberries are store-bought, wash in two waters. Put gooseberries in fermentation vat and mash with pestle (larger amounts can be crushed with a grape crusher). Add pectolytic enzyme and potassium metabisulfite. Pour boiling water on berries to make five gallons. When cool, check with hydrometer. Weigh out enough sugar to obtain reading of 32° Balling. Withdraw one gallon of liquid, heat, and dissolve sugar. Return to fermentation vat and mix thoroughly with must. When temperature reads 70° F, add yeast, cover, and ferment. Stir and measure temperature and sugar content daily. When 10–12° Balling is reached, strain out and press pulp. Rack wine into 5-gallon jug, seal, and allow to continue secondary fermentation until all activity ceases and wine is clear, when it can be bottled.

The Compleat Housewife, from which we quoted earlier, supplies the following recipe for gooseberry wine:

"Take twenty-four quarts of gooseberries, full ripe, and twelve quarts of water, after it has boiled two hours; pick and bruise your gooseberries one by one in a platter with a rolling pin, as little as you can, so they be all bruised; then put the water, when it is cold, on your mashed gooseberries, and let them stand together twelve hours; when you drain it off, be sure to take none but the clear; then measure the liquor, and to every quart of that liquor put three quarters of a pound of fine sugar, the one half loaf sugar; let it stand to dissolve six or eight hours, stirring it two or three times; then put it in your vessels, with two or three spoonfuls of the best new yeast; stop it easy at first, that it may work if it will; when you see it has done working, or will not work, stop it close, and bottle it in frosty weather."

One of the first wines for beginners to try is a wine made from the cranberry juice drink available in most grocery stores. This produces a delightfully piquant, zesty wine that clears rapidly and matures early. For five gallons of this wine you will need:

> 4 gallons Ocean Spray Cranberry Juice Cocktail
> 6 pounds sugar
> 1 package Montrachet dry yeast.

Pour three gallons of cranberry juice into a 5-gallon jug. Empty one gallon into a stainless-steel or unchipped enamel pot. Add sugar, heat, and stir until all dissolved, pour the syrup into 5-gallon jug with the rest of the cranberry juice. When cool (70° F), add yeast, wipe out neck of bottle with paper towel, and plug loosely with sterile cotton wool. Allow to ferment until deposit on bottom of jug is about half an inch thick. Rack into clean 5-gallon jug, and fill to within one inch of brim with additional fresh cranberry juice. Seal with plastic film held down with a rubber band, and allow to continue fermenting until all bubbles stop and wine is sparkling clear; then bottle.

Another cranberry wine, which has more body and needs longer to mature, is made from the fruit itself. By changing the amount of fruit and sugar slightly, either a light dry or full medium wine can be made. This recipe will make five gallons:

> 10 pounds cranberries (12 pounds for medium wine)
> 5 grams pectolytic enzyme
> 3 grams potassium metabisulfite
> 4 ounces fresh ginger root
> 3 pounds chopped raisins
> water to make five gallons

sugar to obtain Balling reading of 24° (30° for medium wine)
1 package Montrachet yeast.

Place cranberries in fermentation vat and crush with pestle.
Add pectolytic enzyme, potassium metabisulfite, bruised ginger root, and well-chopped raisins. Boil two gallons of water
and pour over contents of vat. When cool, add additional
water to make five gallons, stir well, and take hydrometer
reading. Calculate sugar needed to reach a Balling of 24–28°.
Withdraw one gallon of liquid from vat, heat, and add sugar,
stirring until all dissolved. Return syrup to fermentation vat,
stirring so that all contents are completely mixed. When
liquid cools to 70° F, add yeast. Cover and allow to ferment.
Stir and read thermometer and hydrometer daily until Balling
of 4–6° is reached. Strain out raisins, ginger, and cranberry
pulp. Press in a pressing bag and discard. Rack pressed and
free-flow liquid into 5-gallon jug, topping off with cool boiled
water if needed to make liquid level reach to within one to
one and a half inches of brim of jug. Rack as indicated to
remove wine from sediment. When wine is clear and still,
bottle and store until mature. This storage should be for at
least a year. If a somewhat less spicy wine is preferred, the
ginger root can be left out of the recipe.

It is possible that tea wines should have been discussed
with herb wines; however, we have elected to treat them
separately because the method of making these wines is nearly
identical for all of the following: linden flowers and leaves,
mint, maté, sage, and oriental tea. Other leaves that can
be used with this recipe include balm, sweet woodruff, strawberry, and raspberry. For five gallons of wine, the following
ingredients are used:

    5 ounces of dried leaves
    5 pounds of raisins
    12 lemons
    sugar to reach 26–28° Balling

water to make five gallons
1 package Montrachet yeast.

Boil half a gallon of water and pour it over the tea in an enamel pot. Allow it to steep for 8–10 minutes. Chop raisins, and squeeze lemons and grate rinds for their zest. Place chopped raisins, lemon juice, and zest into fermentation vat. Pour over them the strained tea, adding water to bring to five gallons. When cool, take hydrometer reading. Measure sugar needed to obtain 26–28° Balling. Withdraw one gallon of liquid and reheat. Stir in sugar, dissolving completely. Return syrup to fermentation vat, stirring in thoroughly. When mixture has cooled to 70° F, add yeast, cover, and allow to ferment. Stir and read thermometer and hydrometer daily. When hydrometer shows about 4° Balling, strain out raisins and rack into 5-gallon jug, topping off to within one and a half inches of the brim with cool boiled water as necessary. Rack as required to remove clear wine from sediment. Bottle when still and clear. This, like all wines, will improve with age.

One word of caution: When making wine from commercial tea, be sure to use one that appeals to your taste when served hot in the usual manner and has enough flavor to make a tasty wine. Green teas will generally be found to be too bland, while at the other end of the scale such varieties as Lapsang Soochong are much too heavy and smoky to result in a drinkable wine. Also, if the tea is allowed to steep for too long, much tannin will be extracted and a longer period is needed before the wine is drinkable.

In order for wine to age long enough to develop its best qualities it must be stored in sealed, air-tight containers. Wood casks are porous, and while they are valuable as conditioners for wine, they are not suitable for long-time storage of dry wines. In ancient Greece and Rome air-tight amphorae were used for wine storage, and aged wines were as much admired then as they are today. Alexis, the playwright, put it this way:

Man's nature is not at all the same as wine's.
He loses flavor as his life declines;
We drink the oldest wine to come our way;
Old men get nasty, old wine makes us gay.

Recently discovered ships sunk in the Mediterranean two thousand years ago were found to contain ceramic amphorae sealed with pozzuolana, a volcanic-ash cement. The contents of these amphorae were intact, although the wine had changed to a watery substance with a few minerals. Wines stored in such containers were preserved and improved over the years.

With the decline of the Roman Empire, the skill that went into the creation of such admirable wine containers was lost. Wine was still made, but most of it was stored in inadequately stoppered wood casks. Evaporation through wood pores left the wine exposed to air, and it had to be consumed quickly before it turned to vinegar.

This was the golden age of honey wines.

Not only were casks imperfect preservers of wine stored in them, but once they were opened, vinegar developed even faster. In order to slow this process, all sorts of preservatives were used. At the present time, high-proof brandy is added to sherry, port, Malaga, Madeira, and other sweet wines in order to preserve them. In the Middle Ages honey and spices were used to extend the life of wine.

Mead became a popular beverage when it was introduced by Norsemen during their travels. Other variations of honey wine, or grape and fruit wine with honey and spices added, are piment and hippocras, basically wine to which honey and spices were added to disguise the sour taste that developed during cask storage and after the barrels were opened. Metheglin and hydromel are wines made from honey with a generous portion of spices added, while melomel usually refers to wine that develops when honey and fresh fruit juices are fermented together. Clarry was another type of honey wine that was popular during the Middle Ages. As Chaucer says:

"He drinketh ipocras, clarree and vernage
of spyces hote, t'encreasen hir courage."

Hippocras is named after the famous Greek physician, the Father of Medicine. The strainer that removed the spices used in the production of hippocras was traditionally called by alchemists "the sleeve of Hippocrates"; and thus the name was transferred to the wine.

The English Housewife by Gervase Markham, one of the many seventeenth-century cook and recipe books, gives this recipe for "Ipocras."

"Take a bottle of wine, two ounces of good cinamon, ½ ounce of ginger, nine cloves and 6 peppercorns and a nutmeg, and bruise them and put them into wine with some rosemary flowers, and so let them steep all night, and then put sugar, a pound at least, and when it is well settled, let it run through a wollen bag made for that purpose. Thus if your wine be claret, the Ipocras will be red; if white, then of that color also."

From Mackenzie's (1829) *Five Thousand Receipts in All the Useful and Domestic Arts*, we find a recipe for walnut mead:

"To every gallon of water put three pounds and a half of honey, and boil them together three quarters of an hour. Then to every gallon of liquor put about two dozen walnut leaves, pour the boiling liquor on them and let them stand all night. Then take out the leaves, put in a spoonful of yeast, and let it work for two or three days, then make it up, and after it has stood for three months, bottle it."

If this recipe is to be used, the following notes should be kept in mind:

As the honey/water mixture boils, it should be skimmed to remove all froth and scum. Either English (Persian) or black walnut leaves may be used. Slight differences in the ultimate flavor of the wine will result. Some time and trouble can be avoided by placing the leaves in a cheesecloth bag. The wine should ferment until the hydrometer shows zero Balling; then "make it up," that is, fill the jug to within one to one and a half inches of the brim, and seal. The wine should be racked as necessary to remove clear wine from sediment, and bottled when completely still and clear.

Another interesting honey wine is a modification of a recipe for "American Wine," from one Joseph Cooper, Esq., of New Jersey, as recorded in the *Family Receipt Book*, published by Randolph Barnes in 1819. The following ingredients are used:

2 pounds raisins
6 lemons
3 grams potassium metabisulfite
4 gallons sweet cider
honey to give 24° Balling
1 package Montrachet yeast.

Place chopped raisins, and lemons sliced thin, into fermentation vat. Add potassium metabisulfite, and pour cider over. Cover and allow to stand twenty-four hours. Add honey and stir until dissolved. Test with hydrometer, and continue adding honey until hydrometer reads 24° Balling. Add 1 package Montrachet yeast. Cover and allow to ferment. Stir, and read thermometer and hydrometer daily. When Balling reaches zero, strain and transfer to 5-gallon jug, adding water if necessary to fill to within one to one and a half inches of brim. Seal and allow to continue fermentation. Rack as necessary to remove clear wine from sediment. When wine is completely still and sparkling clear, bottle. The wine will improve with age.

This basic formula can be modified to include spices such as cinnamon, nutmeg, allspice, ginger, etc., to make metheglin and hydromel. Fruit juices other than cider, or combinations of other juices and cider, can be used to make melomel.

A recipe that is very similar to the one just quoted and may have been the original source for Mr. Cooper's version, was called "A Rich and Pleasant Wine" and comes from the book called *A New System of Domestic Cookery, Formed upon Principles of Economy*, by A Lady (Mrs. Maria E. Rundell):

"Take new cyder from the press, mix it with as much honey as will support an egg, boil gently fifteen minutes, but not in an iron, brass or copper pot. Skim it well; when cool, let it be tunned, but don't quite fill. In March following, bottle it, and it will be fit to drink in six weeks; but it will be less sweet if kept longer in the cask. You will have a rich and strong wine, and it will keep well. This will serve any culinary purpose which milk or sweet wine is directed for. Honey is a fine ingredient to assist and render palatable, new crabbed austere cyder."

A cookbook used at Mount Vernon during Washington's life has a recipe for metheglin that we have modified for use today:

    3 quarts honey
    16 quarts water
    1½ ounces ginger
    2 pounds raisins (chopped)
    5 grams citric acid
    1 package Montrachet yeast.

Mix honey and water, and add ginger, chopped raisins, and citric acid. Boil until amount is reduced one-third. When cold, put in fermenting vat together with yeast. Ferment until hydrometer reads zero. Rack into 5-gallon jug, adding cool boiled water to fill to within one to one and a half inches of brim. Seal and allow to stand until clear and still. Then it may be bottled.

Mrs. J. C. Croly's *Jennie June's American Cookery Book,* of 1878, gives the following recipe for mead:

"To six gallons of water, add six quarts of strained honey, the yellow rind of two large lemons, pared very thin (or grated), and the whites of three eggs beat to a strong froth. Mix and boil all together three quarters of an hour, skimming it well. Pour into a tub. When lukewarm, add three tablespoonsful of good fresh yeast, cover and leave it to ferment. When it is well worked, pour it into a barrel with lemon peel in the bottom, and let it stand 6 months. It will then be ready to bottle."

Preserves, jams, and wine concentrates can be pressed into service to make attractive, rapidly maturing wines during times when no appropriate fresh fruit is available. These preserved ingredients need not be the most expensive or fanciest brands around; and in fact, for quantities needed for making wine, it is best to try to buy preserves or jams from restaurant-supply houses. For the best wines, select fruits with good natural acid content. These include blackberries, apricots, raspberries, and currants. Concentrates made especially for the amateur wine maker are sold by wine making supply stores. These can be fruit concentrates or wine-grape concentrates made from various *Vitis vinifera* varieties. The best of these concentrates are made by evaporating the excess liquid in a vacuum, capturing the volatile essences by a technique similar to still condensation. These fractions are then put back in the concentrate for maximum flavor. For five gallons of wine made from preserves or jam, the following ingredients are required:

10 pounds of preserves or jam
water to dilute to 24° Balling

10 grams citric acid
1 package Montrachet yeast.

Open preserve cans and empty into fermentation vat. Pour in two gallons boiling water, add acid and stir. When preserves are completely mixed with this water and cool, take hydrometer reading, and calculate how much additional water is needed to reduce the concentration of the preserves to 24° Balling. This can be done by slowly adding water, stirring so that it is completely integrated with the preserves, then testing with the hydrometer until the desired reading is reached, or by using the scale in the Appendix that shows the amount of water required to reduce one gallon of concentrate, jam, or preserves to the desired degree Balling.

Add the water needed to reach 24° Balling, stirring well, then add yeast, cover, and allow to ferment. Stir and test daily until Balling reaches zero, then rack wine off the sediment into a 5-gallon jug. Top off with cool, boiled water, seal, and allow to ferment to dryness. Rack as necessary to clear. When still and sparkling clear, bottle. These wines may be consumed early, but improve with age.

Most wine concentrates are sold in three-quart cans or plastic containers. This is almost the exact amount needed to make five gallons of dry wine. The following ingredients are needed for wine made from concentrates:

1 three-quart can of grape wine concentrate
2 grams potassium metabisulfite
water to make five gallons
sugar to obtain 24° Balling
1 package Montrachet yeast.

Pour the concentrate into the fermentation vat, adding potassium metabisulfite. Add water to make five gallons. Stir until liquids are completely mixed. Take hydrometer reading. Withdraw one gallon of liquid and dissolve necessary sugar completely. Return syrup to fermenting vat, mixing thoroughly, and add yeast. Cover and ferment, stirring daily and checking temperature and hydrometer readings until hydrometer reads zero Balling. Rack into 5-gallon jug, topping off with cool, boiled water as necessary. Seal, and allow secondary fermentation to continue until the wine is dry and completely still and clear. Bottle, and store until the wine is mature. If the flavor of oak is desired, oak chips may be added during the secondary fermentation and allowed to remain in the wine until it is ready to be bottled.

Wine concentrates offer the amateur wine maker an opportunity to produce grape wines when grapes are not available, or when they are as costly as they have been during the recent past. When the cost of concentrates is compared with the price of grapes, either in the field, or picked and delivered, plus the labor of crushing and pressing, it can be seen that these concentrates are bargains.

7

Red Grape Wine,
White Grape Wine,
Sparkling Wines, Sherry

Among all wines, red wines made from superior *Vitis vinifera* varieties command the highest respect. When they are well made and properly aged, they can afford the most supremely satisfying experience in the realm of wine enjoyment.

In this day of heavy commercial demand for wine grapes of all varieties, the amateur wine maker finds himself at a disadvantage having to compete with wineries that are anxious and able to purchase all available supplies. The amateur can try to find small growers who are willing to sell him some grapes, he can grow his own, or he can use concentrates. Pressures are particularly acute on the varieties used for better-quality wines. Supplies of Pinot Noir, Gamay Beaujolais, Petit Syrah and Cabernet Sauvignon from commercial sources are simply not available to amateurs. There are better chances of finding useful amounts of such varieties as Alicante-Bouschet, Carignan, Mission, and other heavy-bearing grapes with little varietal distinctiveness or flavor. A supply of Zinfandel, Barbera, Ruby Cabernet, or Grenache should be regarded as the best *vinifera* available to the average amateur, and purchased without delay.

The author has no experience with native American grapes or hybrids, and those readers living in grape-producing areas in the eastern United States are referred to Philip Wagner's classic *A Wine Grower's Guide* for information on those varieties.

Once obtained, grapes should be handled with as much care and attention as if they were the finest varieties to be found. Carelessness in crushing, fermentation, and processing invites mediocre results and should not be tolerated by any conscientious amateur. The practice of crushing any grape that comes from the field may be acceptable and necessary when tons of grapes are used, but should be avoided by amateurs, who process smaller amounts. The bunches of grapes should be picked over to remove all moldy grapes or those with broken skins. This is a time-consuming task when hundreds of pounds of grapes are involved; however, this is only a small part of the total time required before the wine is enjoyed, and removal of possible sources of spoilage and infection will assure the wine a good beginning.

When the defective grapes have been removed, the remaining fruit can be crushed. At this point the wine maker should decide whether or not stems should be included in the fermenting must. Removal of stems produces a wine that matures more quickly and is smoother and ready for serving a year or more before wines that arc fermented on the stems. On the other hand, wine fermented with the stems is often sturdier and capable of maturing to greater age.

A recommended compromise usually results in a wine that matures somewhat later than wine made without stems but will be able to live to a greater age and derive much benefit in the process. This compromise is to de-stem between a half and three-quarters of the grapes that go into the fermenting vat.

When the grapes have been crushed, potassium metabisulfite is added in the amount of 7.5 grams per 100 pounds of grapes and stirred into the fresh must until it is completely incorporated. At this time a sample of the juice should be tested for sugar and acid balance. Most California grapes, if picked at the proper time, will have sufficient sugar, and may have too much. A more usual deficiency is in acid. If the acid test shows that less than about eight or nine grams per liter of tartaric acid is present, additional acid should be added. Tartaric acid should be used with grape wine rather than malic, citric, or a combination, because it is the acid found naturally in grapes. If tests show an acid level of 5 grams per liter, 3 grams per liter should be added to bring the level to the minimum 8 grams per liter. Tartaric acid in the amount of 3.78 grams to each gallon of wine will increase the level 1 gram per liter. Therefore, for five gallons of must (the quantity most often used in these recipes) to be increased to 8 grams of acid per liter, a total of 3.78 times 3 times 5 grams, or 56.7 grams, of tartaric acid should be dissolved in a small amount of water and stirred into the fresh must.

The must should now be covered and allowed to stand for four to eight hours to allow the potassium metabisulfite to dissipate enough so that yeast growth is not inhibited. After that time, a pure culture of yeast is added. For red wine a good burgundy yeast should be started three days prior to crushing. After the yeast is added, the vat is covered and allowed to stand for twenty-four hours. At this time the must is stirred, the cap pushed down, and temperature and hydrometer readings taken. These steps should continue on a daily basis until the hydrometer reads approximately 6° Balling. At this juncture the wine should be examined for color. If it appears pale, lacking in sufficient depth, and *if the weather is cool*, the wine maker may wish to extract more color and body by allowing the wine to remain on the skins for an additional time. In this case, the wine should be watched very carefully and stirred twice daily until the desired depth of color is obtained. It should be understood that not only will more color be extracted, but greater amounts of tannin and other substances too, so a wine that matures more slowly can be expected to result.

The next step depends upon whether the wine maker wishes

to continue with only free-run wine or a combination of pressed and free-run. As with the decision whether or not to include stems in the must, the wine maker is aware that free-run wine will be smoother and mature more rapidly, while on the other hand lightly pressed must will furnish elements that add body and character to the finished wine. For best results it is recommended that pressed and free-run wine be combined. Another possible alternative, for those interested in obtaining maximum benefit from the grapes available, is to use only free-run wine and chaptalize the remaining unpressed must to make a secondary wine.

Secondary, or chaptalized, wines are made by adding sugar water of the same quantity and Balling degree to the unpressed grape pomace and fermenting this mixture again.

Count Chaptal was a famous chemist who became Minister of Industry and Director General of Commerce and Manufacture under Napoleon I. His advocacy of adding sugar to musts during poor seasons when the vines were unable to generate enough sugar for satisfactory wine resulted in his name being used to describe any wine made with added sugar.

While the amateur wine maker can profitably use the pomace remaining after the free-flow wine has been racked off, he should not try to go as far as a character named Abel Pétiot de Chamiry, who, as reported in *Grape Culture, Wines and Winemaking, with Notes upon Agriculture and Horticulture,* by Agostin Haraszthy, in 1862, made 285 hectoliters of wine that ordinarily would have made only 60 hectoliters, by extending Chaptal's suggestion to the nth degree.

Starting with freshly crushed grapes, he obtained 45 hectoliters of free-run juice. He replaced the juice with 50 hectoliters of sugar water, fermenting the must for three days. This wine was drawn off, and 55 hectoliters of sugar water was added to the hard-working grapes. After two days of fermentation this wine was drawn off, and still a third addition was made. After two more days of fermenting, the wine was finally drawn off and pressed to give 60 hectoliters of wine. The pressed pomace was not allowed to rest on its laurels, but was tossed back into the vat with another 35 hectoliters of sugar water, which added 39 more hectoliters of wine. The entire experiment was capped by adding more sugar water to the first free-run white wine, so that twice as much white wine was produced! Mr. Pétiot was so pleased with the results that the following year he made 5,000 hectoliters in the same manner, although we are not told whether he used the same grapes or gathered some new ones at the next harvest.

In any case, whether the wine is to be free-run or pressed and free-run, the wine is next racked into containers that are filled full and sealed with plastic film or a water seal, and secondary fermentation takes place. Racking is normally conducted twice a year, in the spring and the fall, during the time before bottling. If the wine is stored in oak barrels, it should be topped with similar wine at intervals ranging from every two weeks to every two months, depending upon the size of the barrel and the humidity and temperature of the storage area.

When the wine is sparkling clear and completely still, it can be bottled. For best results, free-run wine should be allowed to mature for three years, while pressed wine should normally rest for five years.

Dr. Chase's Recipes, or Information for Everybody (47th edition, 1867) gives the following red wine recipe:

"Ripe, freshly picked, and selected, tame grapes, 20 pounds; put them into a stone jar and pour over them 6 quarts of boiling soft water; when sufficiently cool to allow it, you will squeeze them thoroughly with the hands; after which allow them to stand three days on the pomace with a cloth thrown over the jar, then squeeze out the juice and add 10 pounds of nice crushed sugar and let it remain a week longer in the jar; then take off the skum, strain and bottle, leaving a vent until done fermenting when strain again and bottle tight, and lay bottles on the side in a cool place."

Dr. Chase then comments on the result of the above recipe: "This wine is the same used by the Rev. Orrin Whitmore of Salina, Mich. for sacramental purposes. I have tasted it myself, and would prefer it for medicinal use to nine-tenths of the wine sold in the country. With age it is nice. I am of the opinion that it might just as well remain in the jar until it is desired to bottle, and thus save the trouble of extra straining. For I have now wine four years old in my cellar. Made in Evansville, Ind. from the grape, which was made without the addition of any particle of matter whatever. Simply the juice pressed out, hauled from the vinery, put into very large casks in a cool cellar, not even racked off again under one year from time of making. It tastes exactly like the grape itself; this, you will perceive, saves much time and trouble in racking, straining, &c. I am told by other winemakers also, that if care is observed when the juice is pressed out to keep clear of the pomace, that wine is better to stand without racking or straining, and that nothing is found in the barrels, after the first year, save crude tartar, or wine-stone, as some call it, which all grape wine deposits on the side of the cask. These wines are in every way appropriate for sacramental and medicinal purposes, and far more pure than can be purchased one in a hundred times, and if one makes their own, they have the satisfaction of *knowing* their wines are not made of what is vulgarly, yet truly called *Rot Gut Whisky*."

Dr. Chase's recipe seems quite adequate for Elvira or Norton or other high acid, eastern grapes. However, his chances of ending up with vinegar seem excellent if he leaves wine in an open stone jar until it is ready to bottle. His barrel of wine might stand a slightly better chance of turning out to be potable if he has a very cold, very damp cellar and a cask with very thick staves, so that little of the wine evaporates and he has a minimum of air space left above the wine.

The Virginia Cookery Book, compiled by Mary Stuart Smith and published in 1885, has an interesting recipe for wine made from Catawba grapes that is prefaced by the following

Traditional grape crusher showing corrugated rollers and spacing to allow seeds to pass between rollers without being crushed.

obeisance to the temperance wave that was sweeping the country at that time: "While the compilers of these recipes advocate the strictest temperance, they do not exclude from their collection directions for making pure wines at home, useful as they are for medicinal purposes, and for making wholesome and palatable some articles of diet. Since Jesus

Christ, our great exemplar, in his intercourse with men, seems to have taught moderation, rather than exclusion of any creature fitted for nourishment from lawful use, we cannot think it wrong to make, or to teach others how to make, pure wine for home consumption."

"Gather the grapes and strip them from their stalks, leaving out all decayed ones; put them into a large china bowl or wooden tub; with a masher break the skins and express the juice; cover so the gnats may not be attracted, and leave for several days, or until decided fermentation sets in; then strain, and to each gallon of the juice put one pound of white sugar. A delicious lady's sweet wine is thus furnished—such as would be very reviving to a delicate or feebled person."

That recipe serves to introduce white grape wine. In making white wine from grapes, the wine maker has greater latitude in his selection of grapes than for red wines. White wine grapes, table grapes, or even grapes ordinarily used for red wines can be used to make white wine. In fact, Pinot Noir, the grape used for the great French burgundies, is also the principal grape used to produce champagne. The same demand for preferred varieties as discussed in the section on red wine holds true for varietal white wines.

The recommendations concerning careful examination and selection of only sound grapes is more important for white wines because of the greater delicacy of the finished wine, in which any trace of moldiness or decay will be quite pronounced.

After the picked-over grapes have been crushed, potassium metabisulfite at the rate of 7.5 grams per 100 pounds of grapes is added. Pectolytic enzyme should be added in the amount recommended by the producer and depending upon the strength of the enzymes used. If red-skinned grapes are used, they should be lightly pressed at once. White-skinned grapes can be allowed to stand for four to six hours to permit the enzymes to break down the pulp of the grapes, resulting in greater juice extraction. In either case, it is recommended that the fresh juice be allowed to stand another four hours after being pressed. This will allow most of the solids in the juice to settle, and basically clear juice to be racked off. Removal of this debris will allow much more rapid clearing of the wine during secondary fermentation. After being racked, the fresh juice should be tested for sugar and acid, and necessary corrections made. After any necessary modifications, the yeast starter should be added and fermentation allowed to proceed.

Daily stirring and testing with thermometer and hydrometer should continue until the hydrometer shows zero Balling. At that time the wine is racked into a closed container and sealed with plastic film or a fermentation lock. The wine should be racked in the spring and the fall until entirely clear and still. It can then be bottled and allowed to mature for one to two years.

Any of the recipes in this book can be modified to produce sparkling wines by reducing the initial sugar content to no more than 20–22° Balling. The wine is then made in the usual manner and allowed to become completely still and clear. The wine should then have about 10–11 per cent alcohol.

Preparation for the bottle fermentation should begin by establishing a yeast starter, using a bottle of Vierka "Perlschaum" or other champagne yeast that adds very little flavor and throws a firm agglutinated sediment. The starter should be commenced about three days prior to actual bottling, so it will be most active when used. This starter is for 5-gallon quantities only.

Withdraw one pint of wine and heat, dissolving two pounds, six ounces of granulated sugar in it to make a syrup. When the syrup is cool, pour into a 5-gallon jug and add a half pint of the yeast starter. Rack the wine into this jug with minimum agitation and aeration of the wine. The flow of the wine should mix the syrup and starter into the wine. When the jug is half to three-quarters full, it can be gently rocked so that further mixing will take place, again with minimum aeration. When the jug is completely full, the wine can then be racked into clean champagne bottles. *NEVER*, under any circumstances, use plain wine or pop bottles! They are simply not strong enough to withstand the pressures developed during bottle fermentation.

When the bottles have been filled to within one inch of the bottom of the cork, they should be corked with highest-quality corks at least one and a half inches long. These should then be tied down with wire. Champagne corks are not advised, because they require a special corking machine. Poly-

Large hand-operated bottle-corking machine. Units of this size are suitable for small commercial winery operations as well as large-scale home wine making.

ethylene stoppers can be used if the wine is stored no more than two years. These should also be wired down.

After the bottles are corked, they should be stored for at least a year and a half to allow full development and some measure of maturity. The bottles should be stored on their sides for the first year. (If polyethylene stoppers are used, this is not necessary.) After that time, bottles that are to be served should be placed upright about six months before they are scheduled to be opened and served. This will allow the sediment that forms during bottle fermentation to fall to the bottom. Every sparkling wine should be served chilled. If the wine in these bottles is carefully poured, and the bottle tilted only once, if possible, the deposit will not be disturbed and only clear, bubbling wine will fill the glasses. *¡Salud!*

When polyethylene stoppers are used, the wine maker may wish to store the bottles upside down, as is the practice in the French champagne process. In this case, the wine should be stored vertically, and not at an angle, as is the practice for champagne remuage. When the wine is to be served, the bottle can be carefully removed to a sink, still upside down, and the stopper twisted loose. The sediment will be forced out, and if the operation is skillfully performed, very little of the wine will be lost, and that remaining in the bottle will be clear.

It is possible to simply add syrup to finished still wine and rebottle it, counting on the yeast remaining in the wine to referment the added syrup. This method, however, is not as reliable as that described above and may result in deposits that are not as firm and will tend to cloud the wine as it is poured.

For amounts of wine less than five gallons, syrup can be made using seven and a half ounces of sugar per gallon of wine to be dosed. This syrup should be added in the amount of three tablespoons per ⅕-gallon bottle.

Sherry is somewhat more complicated and difficult to make than dry table wines, and should be attempted only by experienced wine makers. It can be produced from a number of

The decanted wine ready for tasting.

different basic materials that are essentially neutral in flavor.

Spanish sherry is made principally from Pedro Ximénez and Palomino grapes, with other varieties, such as Castellano, Perruno, and Albillo, contributing small amounts. The grapes are grown in warm country and allowed to become quite sweet. After they are gathered, they are sometimes stored in heaps on grass mats and partially dried. When ready, they are crushed, often by treading with nail-studded boots, then "plastered" with plaster of Paris, which combines with the cream of tartar in the juice to add free acid to the wine, reducing the pH and danger of bacterial contamination.

Free-run and first-press juices are combined and fermented, then classified into the type of sherry they will eventually produce. At this point they are aged, then placed in a *solera*, a series of casks of sherry that are positioned in the stack according to age. The top row contains the youngest wine, while the lower rows contain increasingly older wines. About half of the wine in the lowest row of casks is removed for bottling, with wine from each cask in that row being blended with all other wines in that row. The wine withdrawn for bottling is replaced with wine that is drawn from the second row, all mixed together, as before. The same removal, mixing, and replacement takes place with the upper rows of casks as well. This provides a continuing supply of wines that are blended from many casks and for many years, with resulting uniformity in the finished wine.

In the Jerez area, casks are only partially filled, and exposure to the air allows the *flor* yeast to develop as a film on the wine surface. The film usually begins to grow shortly after fermentation is complete, and remains in the casks for years, dropping to the bottom when too heavy, with new film forming to take its place. It is this film which results in the typical *rancio* flavor of sherry. When the desired characteristics have developed, the wine is withdrawn, filtered, fortified by addition of brandy, and bottled.

It is obvious that this complex process is beyond the capabilities of most amateur wine makers; however, a very acceptable form of simple sherry can be made using the following ingredients and process.

The base material may be any fruit or vegetable that lacks a strong, distinctive flavor of its own. Suggested materials include: Grapes: Pedro Ximénez, Palomino, Thompson seedless, Tokay, etc.; Figs; Honey; Concentrates; Carrots; Dates; Potatoes; Raisins.

For five gallons of wine the recommended quantities are:

> 15 pounds of fruit or vegetables
> 5 pounds chopped raisins (unless grapes are used, then use 20 pounds grapes)
> 3 grams potassium metabisulfite
> 15 grams tartaric acid
> water to make five gallons

sugar to reach 30° Balling
1 package Montrachet yeast
1 bottle *flor* yeast.

Crush fruit, and add chopped raisins, potassium metabisulfite, and tartaric acid. Add boiling water to make up five gallons. When cool, measure with hydrometer to determine Balling. Withdraw one gallon of liquid and add half of the sugar required to reach 30° Balling. Reserve the remaining sugar. Heat liquid and dissolve sugar, return syrup to fermenting vat, and stir well. Cover and allow to cool to 70° F. When this temperature is reached, add Montrachet yeast. Cover and allow to ferment. Take temperature and hydrometer readings daily. Do not allow temperature to rise above 72° F. When hydrometer shows 10° Balling, withdraw one gallon of wine, heat, and stir in balance of sugar until dissolved. When syrup has cooled to 70° F, add to fermentation vat and mix thoroughly. At this time a starter should be made with the *flor* yeast.

When the hydrometer reaches zero, rack wine into two 5-gallon jugs, filling each about half full. Pour half of the flor yeast into each jug, and plug the neck of the jug loosely with sterile cotton wool. Store at optimum temperature of 68° F. In a few weeks, islands of flor film will form on the surface of the wine. It should be allowed to grow undisturbed. If portions break away and drift to the bottom, do not worry. This action is typical, and new film will form to take its place. In three to six months the wine may be racked and bottled. If the wine is to be stored in bottles for any length of time, it may be fortified to 18 per cent alcohol, using the Pearson square to determine the correct amount of brandy or vodka to add to the wine.

If an oak flavor is desired, boiled oak chips can be added to the wine when it is placed in the flor bottles. When carefully made, this wine will be very similar to good Spanish sherry.

8

Some Miscellaneous Recipes

Here are two recipes from *The London Art of Cookery, and Housekeeper's Complete Assistant,* By John Farley, Principal Cook at the London Tavern (7th edition, 1792):

"Put two pounds of brown sugar and a pound of honey to every gallon of water. Boil them half an hour, and take off the skum. Put into the tub a handful of Walnut leaves to every gallon, and pour the liquor on them. Let it stand all night, then take out the leaves and put in half a pint of yeast. Let it work fourteen days, and beat it four or five times a day which will take out the sweetness. Then stop up the cask and let it stand six months."

Readers will recognize the similarity between this recipe and that for walnut mead from Mackenzie's *Five Thousand Receipts,* given earlier. *The London Art of Cookery* has a section devoted to an "Assortment of cheap articles," from which we have selected this recipe:

"Useful family wine may be made of the elder or common birch tree which grows spontaneously in many parts of the country, and is often found on moors or other barren spots of ground. While the sap is rising in the beginning of March, holes should be bored into the body of the tree, and fassets [faucets] of elder placed in them to carry away the liquor. If the tree be large, it may be tapped in several places, and one branch has been known to yield a gallon a day. The sap is boiled with sugar in the proportion of four pounds to a gallon, and to be fermented and treated in the same manner as other home made wines. It is recommended for scorbutic complaints, and other impurities of the blood."

The Experienced English Housekeeper, by Elizabeth Raffald, is the source of this recipe for sycamore wine:

"Take two gallons of the sap and boil it half an hour, then add to it four pounds of fine powdered sugar, beat the whites of three eggs to a froth, and mix them with the liquor, but if it be too hot, it will poach the eggs, skum it very well, and boil it half an hour, then strain it through a hair sieve, and let it stand till next day, then pour it clean from the sediments, put half a pint of good yest to every twelve gallons, cover it close up with blankets, till it is white over, then put it into a barrel, and leave the bung hole open till it has done working, then close it up well, let it stand three months then bottle it, the fifth part of the sugar must be loaf, and if you like raisins they are a great addition to the wine. N.B. You may make birch wine the same way."

Wine made from ripe (orange or red) rose hips is among the most attractive in the wine maker's repertoire. Hips from wild roses, often found along fencerows or bordering streams, make a particularly flavorful wine.

For five gallons of rose-hip wine, the following ingredients are necessary.

15 pounds fresh ripe rose hips or 2 pounds dried rose hips
6 lemons sliced
2 pounds chopped raisins
3 grams potassium metabisulfite
water to make five gallons

sugar to obtain Balling reading of 24°
1 package Montrachet yeast.

Chop or grind fresh rose hips in meat grinder, or chop
dried rose hips small. Add sliced lemons, chopped raisins,
and potassium metabisulfite. Pour two gallons of boiling water over the materials in the fermentaion vat. Add water to
make five gallons. When mixture is cool (70° F), take hydrometer reading and calculate sugar required to reach 24° Balling. Withdraw 1 gallon of liquid, heat and stir in sugar until
a clear syrup results. Pour syrup into fermentaion vat. When
cool, add yeast, cover, and ferment. Take daily readings until
hydrometer reads about 4° Balling. Strain out pulp, press, and
discard. Rack liquid into 5-gallon jug and fill to within one
inch of brim. Seal and allow fermentation to continue until
wine is dry and clear. Rack as necessary to remove from sediment. When wine is bright and still, bottle. Allow to mature for at least a year—then enjoy.

A number of recipes are available for cereal "wines," but it
would appear that most of these are a form of malt liquor,
beer, or ale. The federal regulation concerning wine, §240.352,
C.F.R., makes a statement that appears to be a logical resolution of the identity problem. "Molasses, malts, cereals and
grains may not be used in the production of wine." Of course
this regulation concerns commercial wine making in the
United States, but there appear to be enough other materials
from which to make wine so that cereals can safely be left to
the brewers.

Japanese sake, which is frequently called a wine, yet is
brewed, is made of malted rice grains, cooked rice, and water,
and from these indications should be classified as a non-
carbonated malt brew. In order not to contribute to the con-
fusion, the following recipe uses cracked wheat only as an
adjunct, with other ingredients playing the more prominent
parts in the wine.

For those who like a robust wine high in alcohol, a wine

made from potatoes with the addition of cracked wheat fills the bill:

For five gallons of medium wine the following ingredients are required:

10 pounds potatoes (older ones are fine)
2 pounds cracked wheat
3 pounds raisins (chopped)
6 lemons
6 oranges
3 grams potassium metabisulfite
water to make five gallons
sugar to make 30° Balling
1 package Montrachet yeast.

Scrub the potatoes to remove dirt and grime, and cut out any bruises, scabs, and blemishes. Slice into quarter-inch-thick slices, but do not peel. Add cracked wheat, chopped raisins, and thinly sliced lemons and oranges. Add potassium metabisulfite. Pour boiling water over ingredients to make five gallons. When cool, take hydrometer reading and measure out sugar needed to give 30° Balling. Withdraw one gallon of liquid, heat, and stir in sugar until completely dissolved. Return syrup to fermentation vat, and when mixture cools to 70° F, add yeast and allow to ferment. Stir and measure temperature and Balling daily. Rack as indicated to remove clear wine from sediment. When wine is absolutely still and clear, bottle. Store for no less than a year before using. Never try to substitute buckwheat for the cracked wheat, since it adds an unpleasant, musky flavor to the wine. This wine may be used as a base for sherry.

9

Cooking with and Serving Wine

Sharing wine you have made with family and friends is one of the most rewarding aspects of the wine making hobby. Serving a spectrum of wine of your own making at dinner is no only satisfying to the ego, but offers unusual taste sensations not obtainable from any wine merchant, at any price. Starting with an apéritif of medium-dry elderberry or carrot wine, followed by dinner wines of parsley, cranberry, or plum, and finishing with a dessert wine made of raspberries or potatoes will make any dinner party a success.

In order for each wine to appear at its best and complement the food being served, a few general observations should be kept in mind. These should be regarded as guides rather than absolute rules, and fortunately not even the most snobbish wine "expert" can object to your serving chilled cranberry wine, even if it is red.

Wines usually taste better and go better with the food being served if they are offered and consumed in the following order:

Young wines should be served before old wines.
Dry wines should precede sweet wines.
White wines should come before red wines.
Light-bodied wines precede full, rich wines.

Unless homemade grape wines are being served, and traditional glasses are desired, a general-purpose wineglass of ample size and tulip shape is all that is required. Glassmakers, wine rigmarolists, and etiquette arbiters have not yet established the proper size and shape of glass to be used with quince, dandelion, or pomegranate wine, so what you have is the best.

Traditional wineglasses, especially those used for serving red wines, are very appropriate, having evolved over the years to show wine to best advantage and to present the aroma and bouquet to the nose in the most concentrated manner. The desired glass is made of thin, clear crystal, so it feels good to the touch, is perfectly transparent, and has no decorations to distract the taster from the beauty of the wine itself. It is stemmed to allow the wine to be clearly observed while holding it to the light, and to keep chilled wines from becoming too soon warmed by the hands. The bowl is slightly constricted at the opening to concentrate the fragrance and scents, allowing them to be savored and appreciated.

Greatest appreciation of the bouquet and style of the wine is possible if the glass is filled only about a third full. This allows the evaporating essences to be captured and held within the glass, to be assessed again and again as the tasting goes on. The glass should be of generous size so that even when partially full it will contain several ounces. Wineglasses should have a capacity of no less than eight ounces.

Because home wine makers do not have access to commercial plate filters, and wines are sure to throw a deposit as they mature, it is probably best to decant wines before they are served. If this operation is carefully performed, very little wine is lost, and none will be muddy and bitter from the sediment. To decant a bottle of wine, take the bottle in one hand, holding it close to the bottom. Place a small funnel in the decanter, then place a small light on the other side of the decanter so it will shine through the wine as it is being poured. Slowly and carefully tilt the bottle and allow the wine to run

Traditional wine bottles. Different shapes are associated with various kinds of wine. From left to right: Bordeaux, champagne, champagne magnum, Burgundy (red), Burgundy (white), Rhine (brown glass), and Moselle half bottle (green glass).

into the funnel avoiding all gurgling of the wine at the neck of the bottle, if possible. As the last of the wine is poured, the deposit in the bottom of the bottle will reach the neck. At that point, pouring should stop. The decanter will contain only clear wine, and the amount of wine left in the bottle should be not much more than an ounce. If the wine has been properly stored on its side, it should be brought from the storage place about an hour or two before being served and allowed to stand upright, so the sediment can drop to the bottom of the bottle. If small particles of matter are seen floating in the bottle of wine, a small piece of cotton wool placed in the funnel will strain these out and not damage the taste of the wine.

Wine bottles should be carried from their storage place with great care so that a minimum amount of sediment is stirred up. If the wine is to be chilled, it should be placed in a refrigerator about an hour and a half or two hours before serving. If the cellar is very cool, say around 55° F, red wine should be allowed to slowly reach a temperature of 65° F before serving.

The same general observations that are traditional in serving grape wine with various foods can be applied to wines made from various fruits, tubers, herbs, etc.

Medium-dry wines of good body and some astringency may be served as apéritif wines. Typical of this sort of wine would be one with moderate dryness and the generally robust flavor of a sherry. Such wines can be made from fruits such as pomegranate, date, fig, grapefruit, and elderberry; or flowers such as daisies, marigolds, dandelions, and elder flowers. Carrot wine makes an excellent apéritif when not too sweet, as do wines made from caraway and sage.

For light foods, such as fish or fowl, white wines made from celery, parsley, or tomato are recommended, while for red meat, a light elderberry, dry rose hip, or even currant wine will be acceptable.

Almost any of the fruit or berry wines are excellent for dessert, especially if they are made with a little excess sugar. Amateur wine makers are in a perfect position to establish their own traditions of appropriate food-and-wine combinations. Who knows what food may be perfectly complemented by birch-sap wine or ginger wine? This exploration of new wine-and-food patterns can be a fascinating and rewarding extension of the wine making hobby.

Wine has been an intimate and important part of the art of cooking since time immemorial. Its ability to soften the tough fibers of meat and to complement almost any food have made it a natural and valuable adjunct to cooking. Recipes employing wine are almost always based on the use of grape wines, with certain well-established combinations encountered in almost every cookbook, except those of the nineteenth century in the United States, which were emasculated by the popular prohibitionist movement that ended in the desolate years of the "Great Experiment." One of the first recorded recipes that includes wine in cooking is that for "Wine Cake," given by Cato the Censor in the second century B.C.:

> "Moisten 1 gallon of white wheat flour with wine. Add anise, cumin, a grated twig of bay, two pounds of shortening and a pound of cheese to moisten the flour. Shape the cakes and bake them on a layer of bay leaves."

The *Iliad* tells of a combination of food and wine prepared by Hekamede for Nestor that combines grated goat cheese and white barley in a bowl of Pramnian wine. In the *Odyssey*, Circe puts together a mixture of cheese, barley meal, and yellow honey, flavored once again with Pramnian wine; her objective was not nourishment, however, since she also included a powerful drug to make Odysseus' companions forget their native land.

Eighteenth-century recipes provide an interesting view of the eating habits of that time, together with an opportunity to experiment with and serve dishes that are authentic and tasty reminders of that earlier day. This one is from *The Cook's Paradise, A Complete System of Cookery,* by William Verral, published in 1759:

> "This may be done with peaches of the fleshy sort, and cut in two, put them into some Rhenish wine as long as you please, with plenty of fine sugar, cinnamon and lemon peel, dry 'em and fry without any flour, strain your wine into another stewpan, and boil it to a caromel; dish up and pour it over with the kernels of the peaches blanched, split and thrown in.
>
> "Apricots, or any sort of good large fruit, are done in the way as before, with this difference only; you must be very cautious to use them tenderly, and fry them in a thin batter of small beer and flour: there is a fleshy nectarine

that makes a fritter, but they too must be fried in this batter, for the skin won't bear the violent heat of the lard."

Using any sort of white wine, this recipe provides an interesting dessert. For most fruits, however, the batter of flour and beer is better than simply dropping the fruit into hot fat. It is interesting to note that the same sort of batter using flour and beer is used by Japanese cooks for their *tempura* dishes. Beer makes the batter very tender and crisp and is recommended for all batter dishes instead of water or milk.

From another eighteenth-century cookbook, called *The Compleat Housewife*, which had its fifteenth edition in 1753, we extract the following recipe for "Plum Porridge":

"Take a leg and shin of beef to ten gallons of water, boil it very tender, and when the broth is strong, strain it out, wipe the pot, and put in the broth again; slice six penny loaves thin, cutting off the top and bottom; put some of the liquor to it, cover it up, and let it stand a quarter of an hour, and then put it in your pot; let it boil a quarter of an hour, then put in five pounds of currants; let them boil a little, and put in five pounds of raisins, and two pounds of prunes, and let them boil until they swell, then put in three quarters of an ounce of mace, half an ounce of cloves, two nutmegs, all of them beat fine, and mix it with a little liquor cold, and put them in a very little while, then take off the pot and put in three pounds of sugar, a little salt, a quart of sack, a quart of claret and the juice of two or three lemons; you may thicken with sago instead of bread, if you please; pour them into earthen pans and keep for use."

French cooks use six principal warm sauces as the cornerstones for their cookery. These are espagnole, or brown sauce; velouté, or white sauce; béchamel; allemande; tomato; and hollandaise. From these foundation sauces, about fifty secondary, or "small," sauces are evolved. These include sauce Robert, béarnaise, chasseur, Bordelaise, and many others. More than half of those call for the use of wine. Some of the better-known sauces are given recipes in the classic *Guide Culinaire*, by A. Escoffier:

Sauce Bordelaise

INGREDIENTS:
> ½ pint red wine, the best you can spare
> 2 ounces minced shallots
> pinch of pepper
> pinch of thyme
> bay leaf
> meat glaze (consommé)
> lemon juice
> 4 ounces beef marrow (chopped)
> 3 ounces butter.

Place wine in saucepan, add shallots, pepper, thyme, and bay leaf, reduce wine by three-fourths and add consommé, simmer for half an hour, and strain through a napkin or a sieve. Add lemon juice and the marrow, which has previously been simmered in slightly salted water. Smooth out with added butter.

Sauce Chasseur

INGREDIENTS:
> 6 medium-sized mushrooms, peeled and chopped
> ½ ounce butter
> ½ ounce olive oil
> 1 teaspoon chopped shallots
> ½ pint white wine
> 1 glass brandy
> ½ pint consommé
> ¼ pint tomato sauce
> 1 tsp chopped parsley.

Heat butter and oil in saucepan, add chopped mushrooms, browning rapidly. Add shallots, and then remove half of the butter and oil. Pour the wine and brandy into the saucepan, reduce to half, and add consommé and tomato sauce. Boil for 5 minutes and add chopped parsley to finish.

Sauce Robert

INGREDIENTS:

> 1 large onion
> 4 tablespoons butter
> ½ teaspoon salt
> ⅔ cup white wine
> 1 cup consommé
> 1 teaspoon dry mustard
> 1 pinch powdered sugar.

Chop the onion fine and simmer in butter until golden. Add salt, combine wine and consommé, and cook until reduced one-half. Add this to the onion and cook slowly for 30 minutes. Stir in mustard and sugar just before serving. Do not cook after the mustard has been added, but you may keep the sauce warm in a double boiler if necessary.

Sauce Robert was invented sometime during the fourteenth century, and has remained a standard sauce in the cook's repertoire ever since.

Pork chops are vastly improved by the use of white wine:

> 4 one-inch-thick loin pork chops
> 1 teaspoon dried rumbled sage leaves
> 1 teaspoon dried rumbled rosemary leaves
> 1 teaspoon finely chopped garlic
> 1 teaspoon salt
> ½ teaspoon freshly ground pepper
> 2 tablespoons butter
> 1 tablespoon olive oil

¾ cup white wine
1 tablespoon chopped parsley.

Combine sage, rosemary, garlic, salt, and pepper and press into both sides of each pork chop. In a heavy skillet melt the butter and oil over moderate heat. When foam subsides, place chops in hot fat and brown two to three minutes on each side, turning with tongs to avoid puncturing the chops. When they are golden brown, remove. Pour off all but a small amount of the fat, add a half cup of wine and bring to a boil. Return chops to pan, cover, and reduce heat until liquid barely simmers. Cook chops twenty-five to thirty minutes, basting frequently. Transfer to warm serving platter, and place in warm oven. Add remaining wine to pan, boil over high heat, stirring constantly until reduced to glaze. Taste and adjust, add chopped parsley, and pour over chops, serving immediately.

This Italian recipe, called Maiale Chianti, also combines pork and wine. It appears to have originated in the vicinity of Lucca sometime before the telescope was invented by Galileo in neighboring Pisa.

INGREDIENTS:

5 pounds boneless pork shoulder
large clove garlic
1 tablespoon flour
1 teaspoon salt
½ teaspoon dried crumbled oregano (or marjoram)
¼ teaspoon dried crumbled rosemary leaves
6 cloves
bay leaf
2 cups Chianti or other light red wine.

Chop the garlic very fine, and mix together with flour, salt, oregano, and rosemary. Sprinkle over meat, and press into meat. Pierce meat with the cloves and lay the bay leaf on top. Bake in a shallow baking dish for three to four hours at 300°, basting frequently with the wine. When cooked, remove meat from pan to warm oven. Remove most of the fat from the pan, add 1 cup wine, cook briskly until thick, then replace meat in pan, spoon sauce over the meat, and serve.

An unusual recipe for wine soup comes to us from the Austro-Hungarian Empire. This Viennese recipe for Wein Suppe calls for the following ingredients:

3 cups dry white wine
1 cup water
1 stick cinnamon
sugar to taste
4 egg yolks
1 teaspoon flour
2 tablespoons butter
toasted Semmelen slices (white bread).

Heat the wine and water together with the stick of cinnamon, and sugar to taste; when this has been well mixed together, one boils four egg yolks and the flour with some cold wine, adding this to the hot wine a little at a time, until thoroughly mixed. When the mixture has simmered for a few minutes, add the butter and stir thoroughly. Serve with toasted Semmelen slices.

A meal started with that wine soup could very well finish with a specialty of Viennese cooking called Weinchaudeau, which calls for the following ingredients:

4 egg yolks
½ cup sugar
1 cup dry white wine.

Combine ingredients in the top of a 1½-quart double boiler. Beat until eggs are pale yellow and fluffy as water simmers in the bottom part of the double boiler. Spoon off the thick part that rises to the top as the mixture is heated and whipped. Fill six punch glasses with the mixture and serve hot.

Charles Francatelli, who was chief cook to Queen Victoria, was lavish in his use of wine. His recipe for Small Ribs of Beef à la Mode requires more preparation than does a frozen dinner, but the results are magnificent!

INGREDIENTS:

    2 slices of ham
    truffles
    3 small ribs of beef
    3 carrots
    3 onions
    2 heads celery
    ½ bunch parsley
    2 cloves garlic
    6 cloves
    2 blades mace
    1 bottle sherry
    2 glasses brandy
    1 cup consommé.

Trim and daube (interlard) with ham and truffles three small ribs of beef; prepare them for braising with the trimmings and the vegetables. Moisten with a bottle of sherry and two wineglassfuls of brandy; then set the pan containing the ribs of beef on the stove fire and simmer about a quarter of an hour; after which add the consommé, cover the whole with buttered paper and the lid, return the pan to the fire, and allow to continue gently simmering for three or four hours—according to the weight or size of the piece of beef. When done, drain and trim it, place it in a saucepan with a little of its own liquor; put it into the oven to dry a minute or two previous to glazing it; unless, indeed, it has already been glazed during the latter part of the braising, which is the better method—frequent basting with its own liquor imparting additional flavor; when glazed, dish the ribs of beef up, and garnish them around with groups of glazed carrots and onions; sauce around with the essence in which the beef has been braised, clarified, and boiled down to the consistency of a half glaze for the purpose, and serve.

A much simpler recipe, but one that is extremely effective with almost any delicately flavored fish, such as sole, halibut, or swordfish, uses the following ingredients:

4 tablespoons butter
2 tablespoons chopped parsley
2 tablespoons chopped shallots or onions
½ cup white wine (the best you can spare)
1 teaspoon salt
½ teaspoon fresh ground pepper
¼ cup bread crumbs
1 tablespoon soy sauce
juice of ½ lemon.

Melt half the butter and place in a shallow baking pan. Add half the chopped parsley and shallots. Place the fish on these, pour over the fish the remaining butter, shallots, and parsley, spreading to cover the entire fish. Cover with white wine, pouring carefully so as not to disturb the shallots and parsley. Sprinkle the salt, pepper, and breadcrumbs over the top of the fish. Bake between fifteen and twenty-five minutes, depending upon thickness of the fish, at 350°. Strain liquid from the fish, setting them aside in the oven to keep warm. Add soy sauce to liquid and reduce to half, thicken with corn starch, but do not boil. Add lemon juice. Pour over fish, and brown quickly under broiler and serve.

Although Bercy sauce was originally developed for fish, this version has been adapted for meat, in the following recipe for Steak Bercy.

INGREDIENTS:

1 steak, one inch thick
4 tablespoons butter
1 tablespoon finest olive oil
½ pint red wine
3 tablespoons shallots
1 teaspoon salt
½ teaspoon freshly ground pepper
¼ cup consommé
¼ cup chopped marrow
¼ lemon
3 tablespoons chopped parsley.

Heat butter and oil until sizzling hot, put in steak, and brown on both sides; then remove to warm oven. Add wine, chopped shallots, salt, and pepper to pan, and simmer until reduced to a quarter of original volume. Skim surplus fat, add consommé and chopped marrow, cook another eight minutes, taste, and correct seasoning. Squeeze lemon quarter and twist peel over sauce, add chopped parsley, and return steak to pan. Heat until very hot, then serve.

Pears Zinfandel is a pleasant dessert. Peel, halve, and remove cores from desired number of ripe pears. Cover with Zinfandel or other robust red wine until wine is a quarter inch over tops of pears. Add sugar to taste, and simmer over low heat until most of wine is absorbed. Remove to refrigerator and serve quite cold.

This Easy Wine Cake is one of my wife's (and my) favorite recipes. For it the following ingredients are needed:

1 package yellow cake mix (1 pound, 3 ounces)
1 package vanilla instant pudding (4½ ounces)
¾ cup oil
¾ cup sherry, Madeira, or Marsala
4 eggs
1 teaspoon nutmeg
½ cup raisins soaked in sherry until plump.

Preheat oven to 350°.

Combine all ingredients except raisins in bowl and mix with electric mixer set at medium, for five minutes. Add raisins. Pour batter into greased angel-food cake pan. Bake at 350° for forty-five minutes to one hour, until done. Sprinkle with powdered sugar. Nuts may also be added.

Returning to Sir Hugh Plat's *Delights for Ladies*, published in 1609, we find the following recipe that would be useful today to serve with chicken or turkey: "To make a Cullis [strong broth] as white as snow, and in the nature of a Gellie

"Take a cocke, scalde, wash and draw him cleane, seeth it in white or Rhenish wine, skum it cleane, clarifie the broth after it is strained, then take a pint of thicke and sweet creame, strain that to your clarified broth, and your broth will become exceedingly faire and white; then take powdered ginger, fine white sugar and Rosewater, seething your cullis when you season it, to make it take the colour the better."

Another recipe from the same source tells how to "Boil a flounder in the French Fashion:

"Take a pint of white wine, the tops of young thyme and Rosemarie, a little whole mace, a little whole pepper, season with verjuice [vinegar will do], salt and a peece of sweet butter, and so serve it. This broth will serve to boile fish twice or thrice in."

William Verral, who was master of the White Hart Inn in Lewes, Sussex, wrote an extremely sophisticated cookbook in 1759, which has already been referred to as *The Cook's Paradise, A Complete System of Cookery*. From it I have extracted this useful recipe for "Roasted Ham":

"For this entree is generally provided a new Westphalia or Bayonne ham, soaked two or three days in milk and water, and with a handful of coriander seeds; put it to a slowish fire, and baste it with a little Rhenish or other white wine pretty constantly till it is done; but before you spit it draw your knife round between the fat and the sward [rind]; and in roasting you may easily take it all off; make it of a nice colour, and for your sauce dash into it a ladle or two of your cullis [use consommé] a glass of Champagne or Rhenish, and a few tops of Asparagus, cauliflower, or capers, add the juice of a lemon, and serve it up hot."

The recipe for ham is followed by another that can be adapted to present-day dinners. It is called a "Fricassee of Mushrooms":

"Clean some nice button mushrooms with flannel and water, wash them in a second water, and put them into a stewpan with a glass of Champagne, Rhenish or other white wine, a bunch of onions, thyme and parsley, pepper, salt and a blade of mace, toss them up in this upon a stove a few minutes, and pour in a small ladle of broth, with a bit of butter mixt with flour; let all stew a quarter of an hour, take out your herbs, have ready a liaison [thickening] as before, and just before your dinner time, pour it in, move it gently over the stove a minute, squeeze in an orange or lemon, and dish it up."

Elizabeth Raffald, who was married only four years after Verral's book was published in a single edition, and lived to see about eight of the thirteen editions of her *Experienced English Housekeeper*, gives the following recipe for "A Nice Sauce for Most Sorts of Fish":

"Take a little gravy made of either veal or mutton, put to it a little of the water that drains from your fish, when it is boiled enough put it in a sauce pan, and put in a whole onion, one anchovy, a spoonful of catchup, and a glass of white wine, thicken it with a good lump of butter rolled in flour, and a spoonful of cream; if you have oysters, cockles or shrimps, put them in after you take it off the fire, (but it is very good without) you may use red wine instead of white by leaving out the cream."

Mrs. Raffald also gives the following recipe "To Stew Oysters, Cockels and Muscles":

"Open your fish clean from the shell, save the liquor, let it stand to settle, then strain it through a hair sieve, and put to it as many crumbs of bread as will make it pretty thick, and boil them well together before you put in the fish, with a good lump of butter, pepper, and salt to your taste, give them a single boil and serve them up.—N.B. You may make it a fish sauce by adding a glass of white wine just before you take it off the fire, and leaving out the crumbs of bread.

About fifty years later this interesting recipe for Chocolate Wine appeared in the *Cook's Own Book*, of 1835:

"Take a pint of sherry, or a pint and a half of port, four ounces and a half of chocolate, six ounces of fine sugar, and half an ounce of white starch; mix dissolve and boil all these together for about ten or twelve minutes. But if your chocolate is made with sugar, take double the quantity of chocolate and half the quantity of sugar."

Finally, here is my own special recipe for carrots—Carrots Auf der Heide:

Clean and slice carrots, melt 3 tablespoons butter in a saucepan with close fitting cover, add carrots, salt to taste, and cover, simmering slowly in butter. When carrots are nearly done, add ¼ cup of sweet white wine such as sherry, Madeira, etc. Finish cooking carrots. Sprinkle with 1 teaspoon grated tangerine rind. If tangerines are out of season, use dried rind grated, but add with the wine.

10

Questions and Answers

These are typical questions asked by students in my wine making classes. They are included because they may pinpoint specific problems met by beginners in the craft of wine making.

Q. Can pasteurized juices be used for wine making?

A. Pasteurization is a technique of raising the temperature of a food product to a point sufficiently high to destroy most active organisms, but not high enough to destroy spores or to radically change the flavor of the material being pasteurized. This means that pasteurized juices will make good wines if they possess the proper balance of sugar and acid, and are inoculated with a pure strain of active yeast. A distinction should be made between pasteurization, and sterilization by means of various chemicals. Juices containing sorbates, sulfur compounds, or other microorganism inhibitors probably cannot easily be fermented. Read the labels to avoid disappointment when fruit juices, purées, or preserves are used to make wine.

Q. Should I buy a wine making kit?

A. There are almost as many wine making kits as there are suppliers of wine making materials. The usefulness of any wine making kit depends primarily upon individual needs. Some kits actually consist entirely of equipment, with no materials supplied with the package. Others supply almost everything necessary to make a batch of wine. A full description of the kit's contents is needed to determine if it will fit individual requirements. Here is a list of items found in a typical five-gallon kit for beginners, which retails for about $25:

2 air locks	$ 1.60
5 pounds corn sugar	.80
1 gallon fruit concentrate	4.35
15 sodium bisulfite tablets	.95
2 five-gallon jugs	
1 racking tube with siphon assembly	1.00
15 yeast nutrient tablets	.60
1 ounce tartaric acid	.30
1 package Montrachet yeast	.40
	10.00

Subtracting the costs for each item except the five-gallon jugs we come out with the following results:

Total kit cost	$25.00
Cost of all but five-gallon jugs	−10.00
five-gallon jugs	15.00

Jugs such as those provided in this kit can be purchased from local bottled-water dealers for about three dollars each. In addition, shipping weight can be reduced from about fifty pounds to closer to ten pounds with a saving of three dollars, while the chances of breakage are considerably lessened. It appears obvious that the convenience of a wine making kit approximately doubles the cost of individual assembly.

Traditional wineglasses in crystal-clear, unadorned glass. From left to right: sherry, Burgundy, Rhine, champagne, and claret.

Q. Is there any chance that the alcohol generated during wine making can become a fire hazard?

A. The maximum amount of alcohol that can be fermented under ordinary circumstances is about 16 per cent. This means that 84 per cent of the wine volume is water. This ratio effectively prevents any of the alcohol from burning. In addition, at least during fermentation, carbon dioxide is formed. This is an excellent fire-extinguishing material.

Q. If you don't have a hydrometer, how can you tell when the primary fermentation is finished?

A. Primary fermentation is often called active fermentation to distinguish it from slow, or secondary, fermentation. Without a hydrometer, it is usually easiest to tell when the most active stage of fermentation has stopped by looking at the wine. If it no longer froths and bubbles, and when the third or fourth day of violent activity has passed, then the secondary fermentation can safely be started. Some wine makers, especially when making red grape wines, use the color of the wine to indicate when the pomace should be pressed and secondary fermentation allowed to commence. Recipes that specify when to stop the first stage of fermentation suggest intervals of from two days to two months. As far as the wine itself is concerned, fermentation is a process that will continue until all sugar is fermented out, unless the yeast is killed. The wine maker usually removes as much solid matter as possible as soon as he feels the wine will improve with its removal. Usually wine clears faster, matures earlier, and has less chance to spoil and develop off flavors, when the solid matter has been removed. As a rule of thumb, three days of active, violent fermentation are usually sufficient for most purposes, and after that time the danger of trouble increases disproportionately.

Q. How does one know when to rack wine?

A. Racking wine accomplishes two principal ends: 1. The clear wine is removed from contact with dead yeast cells that may be hydrolized and yield unpleasant flavors if allowed to remain in contact with the wine. There are exceptions to this rule, notably in the case of sherry, in which not only is the wine allowed to remain in contact with the yeast for long periods, but the same yeast is used over long periods, sometimes for years, in order to develop the familiar *rancio* sherry flavor. 2. Turbid particles that are deposited with the yeast cells are also removed from contact with the wine, thus preventing their being stirred up when wine is moved from one location to another. Each time wine is racked, it is subject to a certain amount of aeration, and the wine maker must determine whether it is better to allow the lees to accumulate or to remove them and risk overaerating the wine. Usually it is best to handle light, fruity white wines as little as possible, while robust red wines may withstand relatively more aeration without noticeable modification of the character of the wine. As a general rule, for a five-gallon batch of wine the first racking should take place about thirty days after secondary fermentation has started, or when there is approximately an inch of sediment on the bottom of the jug, whichever is earlier. The second racking can be made from sixty to ninety days after the first, or when between one half and three quarters inch of sediment is visible. A third racking can usually follow, six months later. If the sediment deposited after the third racking is not significant and the wine becomes perfectly clear, a fourth racking is usually not necessary.

Q. How long should you wait before drinking wine?

A. Understanding the desire to sample the results of one's efforts, the logical response is to wait as long as possible. In all probability, early wine making efforts will all be consumed before they have a chance to mature. Most fruit wines can be consumed with pleasure after they have aged for a year. They will improve if allowed to rest for a second and a third year. Certain kinds of fruits make wines that require a great deal of aging. Elderberry wine, for example, requires from three to five years in the bottle before it begins to lose its harshness and develop mellowness. Wines made from commercial fruit juices or concentrates may be potable as early as six months after they are made. It is suggested that half of each batch of wine be set aside to mature for at least two years, and if indicated, for an even longer rest.

Q. What causes hangovers?

A. Drinking too much! Alcohol is a poison, just as is, for example, salt. In moderate quantities, either of these substances stimulates the appetite and improves the flavor of food. In larger quantities, either substance can produce unpleasant effects; if it is consumed in sufficient amounts, death can result.

Headaches and gastric distress are frequently encountered after a sufficient amount of wine has been consumed. Some of these effects seem to depend upon the type of wine consumed, the amount and kind of food eaten with the wine, and the general physical condition of the consumer. Heavy, aromatic, dessert-type wines have a relatively large percentage of higher alcohols, and have a narcotic effect on the human organism. Another probable cause for the symptoms of hangover found when drinking wine is the amount of sulfurous acid remaining in the wine due to use of excess sulfur dioxide for preservation. Some wineries use sulfur dioxide too liberally in an attempt to correct problems brought about by inadequate sanitation techniques. Human tolerance of sulfurous acid varies widely from person to person, and certain individuals are much more susceptible to its influence than others.

A 1965 article on the toxicity of wine by P. Marquardt and H. W. J. Werringloer, of the University of Freiburg, discloses that examination of about 120 wines from Europe, North Africa, and Chile indicates the presence of histamines in amounts up to twenty-two milligrams per liter. On the other hand, no histamines were found in fresh musts. The symptoms of the presence of histamines in the body are those traditionally associated with overindulgence in wine: headache, reddening of the face, fall in blood pressure, rapid heartbeat, and a burning sensation in the stomach, often followed by vomiting.

Histamines, according to the authors, are produced by lactobacilli, which are also responsible for converting wine's malic acid into lactic acid, a process encouraged by many European wine makers and tolerated by most wine makers everywhere, because the high acid content of wines grown in cool climates is reduced by conversion of the more sour malic into less sour lactic acid. Other changes that benefit the wine flavor also result from malo-lactic fermentation.

Little attention appears to have been given to the problem of acute and chronic toxicity caused by excessive consumption of wine. If Marquardt and Werringloer's conclusions that histamines are responsible for hangovers and long-term effects such as hepatic cirrhosis, and the presence of histamines in wine are due to bacterial infection of the wine, then the present commercial practice of encouraging malo-lactic fermentation should be re-examined, especially by California vintners, who in our warm land ordinarily do not encounter high-acid musts typical of the cooler climates of Europe.

Home wine makers can reduce the possibility of malo-lactic fermentation by racking immediately after fermentation, careful attention to sanitation, and the addition of moderate amounts of sulfur dioxide to the wine.

Q. Does the color of the glass in the bottles have any effect on wine?

A. Wine is definitely changed by light, and for the best safeguard a dark-green or chestnut (brownish green) bottle is preferred. Chestnut-colored bottles reduce undesirable photochemical changes, because they filter out more light in the ultraviolet region than do bottles of other colors or without color.

Q. Are there any chances of spoiled wine making one sick the way spoiled food does?

A. Fortunately, most wine diseases change the flavor of the wine so that the taste or smell of the wine gives ample warning that all is not well. Infected wine will smell musty, mousy, sour, or unpleasant in other ways, and when tasted will give unmistakable evidence that it has gone bad. Other than unpleasant odors and taste, spoiled wine does not appear to have any dangerous effects as spoiled food can.

Q. Is it all right to use unboiled tap water?

A. In most cities in this country, water from the tap is pure enough so that it may be used without boiling. In some localities, water contains large amounts of minerals, including sulfur and even chlorine, that can flavor the wine. In these locations it is better to use bottled or boiled water for making wine.

Q. Why do you need an open vessel for one fermentation and a closed jug for the second; couldn't the same jug be used for both?

A. Actually, fermentation can be conducted in any container that is inert and of adequate size. An open container is easier to fill and empty, particularly if pulp, skins, etc., are being fermented. About 25 per cent of extra space is required during active fermentation so the froth will be contained within the fermentation vat. If primary fermentation is conducted in a bottle, the wine should, in any case, be transferred to another bottle at the end of primary fermentation. Secondary fermentation should always be conducted in a bottle or other container that is completely filled.

Q. I have some peach wine that will not clear, even though I have tried whites of eggs, gelatin, and bentonite. Nothing seems to work. The wine tastes pretty good, but it is cloudy. What do you suggest I do?

A. Sometimes wine will have a persistent haze that can be cleared only by being passed through a filter press containing bentonite or sheets of asbestos. Home wine makers have nothing available that will do the job without aerating the wine dangerously. There are two solutions available: 1. Pour the wine down the drain or drink it haze and all. 2. Convert the wine to eau de vie, or brandy. Distilling is not legal at home, since the Treasury Department wants taxes paid on all distilled liquors and requires licenses, bonds, and extensive records. If one lives in a cold enough climate, the wine can be placed in a plastic container, with the top covered with plastic film. Left out in the cold overnight, most of the water will solidify, leaving clear, concentrated brandy. Discard the frozen water and repeat the process a second night for best results. This will accomplish the same results as distillation, and not even the Treasury Department can stop the weather. In warmer climates a deep freezer will give the same results.

Q. Can yeast be used more than one time?

A. Yeast can be used for several fermentations if the proper precautions are used and the yeast is kept free from contamination. It is best to throw out the yeast deposited during primary fermentation, and save that yeast deposited during secondary fermentation. This yeast is comparatively free from other materials. If it is to be used within a short time, it can be stored in a sterile glass container in the refrigerator. When the yeast is to be used again, the cover should be loosened and the yeast allowed to return to room temperature for several hours before being added to the must. If the yeast is more than a few months old, it may be well to make a "starter" to see if it has retained its viability during storage.

Here is a recipe for preserving yeast; it comes from Maria Rundell's *A New System of Domestic Cookery, Formed upon Principles of Economy*, by A Lady, published in London in 1808.

"When you have plenty of yeast, begin to save it in the following manner; whisk it until it becomes thin, then take a large, new wooden dish, wash it very nicely, and when quite dry, lay a layer of yeast over the inside with a soft brush; let it dry, then put another layer in the same manner, and do so until you have a sufficient quantity, observing that each coat dry thoroughly before another be added. It may be put on two or three inches thick and will keep several months; when to be used, cut a piece out; stir it in warm water."

Q. When the wine is to be separated from the pulp for pressing, is it best to siphon the liquid out or to dip the pulp out?

A. I have always found it best to dip as much of the solid matter out of the vat as possible before trying to rack out the remaining liquid. This reduces the number of times that the siphon tube is plugged by particles of skin or pulp.

Q. Are there any types of wines that will not be improved by aging?

A. Most dry white tables wines and rosé wines depend almost entirely on their fresh fruity flavor for their appeal. These, and many other fruit wines, are most attractive when they are youthful and sprightly, and are best drunk when they are less than three years old. Almost any wine will need a year or more to shed yeastiness and adolescent brashness. Beyond that time, however, little improvement is obtained by aging fruit wine unless it is very robust and contains a great deal of tannin.

Glossary

ACETIC ACID: The colorless pungent acid that gives vinegar its sharp taste. The next step after alcohol in the uninterrupted fermentation cycle.

ACIDITY: *Total*—All the acid to be found in wine: fixed acids, volatile acids, and carbonic acid. *Fixed*—The acids derived from the fruit, usually tartaric, malic, or citric. *Volatile*—Acids developed during fermentation, such as acetic, lactic, butyric, etc.

AERATION: Addition of air to wine, usually during cellar operations such as racking, filtering, etc.

AGING: The time allocated to wine for development of bouquet. This ordinarily varies with the harshness and astringency of the new wine.

ALCOHOL: The component of wine that stimulates the human organism. It is not the attribute most valued in wine.

AMELIORATION: Addition of substances to wine to improve the end product. This is ordinarily sugar in the case of wines lacking sufficient natural sugar, and water and acid in musts with too much sugar.

AROMA: The distinctive fragrance of the wine making material and the young wine made from it. Not to be confused with bouquet, which see.

BALLING: Measurement of sugar in must. One degree Balling of sugar will ferment out to approximately 50 per cent alcohol and

49 per cent carbon dioxide, depending upon a variety of factors such as temperature, exposure to air, etc. The Gay-Lussac equation indicates the general process involved:

$$C_6H_{12}O_6 = 2C_2H_5OH + 2CO_2.$$

One molecule of sugar will give two molecules of ethyl alcohol and two molecules of carbon dioxide. Balling measurement is a convenient way to determine the potential amount of alcohol that will be produced by a must containing a certain amount of sugar. Brix degrees are identical with Balling, and are often used interchangeably.

BODY: The substances present in wines that have been extracted during fermentation. Wine fermented for longer periods in contact with the pulp and skins usually has more body than wine pressed after a brief active fermentation period.

BOUQUET: The fragrances developed in wine during the process of aging and maturing. An extremely complex spectrum of volatile essences blended and intermingled to provide the culminating objective of the wine maker.

BRIX: Measurement of sugar content of must. See Balling.

BURGUNDY: A robust red wine originally grown on the banks of the Saône River, in what is now the Department of Côte-d'Or, in France. Red Burgundy wines are made from the following grapes, which are allowed in wines having the controlled appellation: Pinot Noir, Pinot Gris, Gamay Noir (with white juice). White Burgundy is made from the following grapes: Pinot Chardonnay, Aligoté, Melon, and Pinot Blanc. Other grape varieties are used, but not in wines that are made with controlled place names.

CHABLIS: The name of a commune in France near the town of Auxerre which has given its name to a famous white wine made from Pinot Chardonnay, Gamay Noir à jus blanc, Pinot Blanc, and Pinot Gris.

CHAMPAGNE: A sparkling white wine developed by secondary fermentation in the bottle. Originally applied to wine made from Pinot Noir, Pinot Blanc, Pinot Gris, and Chardonnay grapes. Now applied to almost any sparkling white wine.

CHAPEAU: (Cap) The layer of light pulp, skins, stems, etc., that rises to the surface of actively fermenting must. It can be a source for development of vinegar-producing bacteria unless frequently submerged in the liquid, pushed down under the surface.

CONCENTRATE: Partly dehydrated must from grapes or other fruit that is reconstituted with water, to be then fermented into wine.

CORKINESS: An off odor present in wines stoppered with decayed corks. If the cork smells like cork instead of like the wine, the cork has gone bad and the wine is spoiled.

CUVÉE: Literally, a cask. A combination of wines, a blend of various wines either from one batch or from different fermentations.

DECANT: Pour wine carefully from the original bottle into a fresh container. Wine is usually decanted just before being served, to remove the clear liquid from deposits that have accumulated in the bottle while the wine was maturing.

DEPOSIT: The sediment thrown off by wine as it ages. The reason for decanting.

DRY: In wines, the opposite of sweet. Wines fermented to dryness have no remaining unfermented sugar. Dry wines are not sour; acid wines are sour.

EFFERVESCENCE: The carbon dioxide bubbles absorbed and retained in the wine during secondary fermentation; they are released when the wine is opened.

ENZYMES: Proteins formed by living cells that can increase the speed of specific reactions of a single type, or small group, of molecules.

FIFTH: One-fifth of a gallon, a common bottle size.

FINING: A method of clarifying wine. Materials used in fining attach themselves to haze-causing particles and sink to the bottom of the container.

FLATNESS: Wine that has lost its verve and tastes bland is called flat. This condition is often found in wines lacking acid.

FLOWERS OF WINE: A disease of wine characterized by dusty white islands floating on the surface of the wine. Usually develops in the presence of air in wines of low alcohol content. Caused by a yeast named *Candida mycoderma,* and should not be confused with the sherry *flor* yeast *Saccharomyces beticus.*

FORTIFICATION: Addition of brandy or other forms of concentrated alcohol to wines in order to prevent spoilage.

FOXINESS: Wine made from grapes containing large amounts of methyl anthranilate, such as Norton, Concord, etc.

GALLON: In the United States, a measure containing 3.78533 liters, or 128 fluid ounces. The imperial gallon, used in the British Commonwealth, contains 153.6 fluid ounces. All measurements in this book refer to U.S. gallons.

HYDROMETER: A thin glass tube, closed at both ends and enlarged and weighted at one end. Used to measure the specific gravity of liquids. The most useful types for wine making have two or more scales: degrees of sugar (Balling or Brix), percentage of potential alcohol, and specific gravity.

HYDROMETER JAR: A narrow glass or plastic tube into which the liquid to be tested is poured. The hydrometer floats in the liquid at a point that indicates the amount of solid matter (usually sugar) contained in the fluid.

ISINGLASS: A highly purified form of fish glue used to fine wines.

LEES: The sediment and accumulated material deposited during fermentation.

MARC: The semi-dry pulp and skins left after pressing.

MUST: Grape or other fruit juice.

PASTEURIZATION: A method of sterilizing wines by heating them to about 145° F to kill yeasts and spores.

PRESS JUICE: Wine extracted by pressing the pomace.

RACK: To remove the (relatively) clear wine from its sediment by siphoning or pumping.

RHINE (RHENISH) WINE: Wine (nearly always white) grown along the Rhine River, in Germany, usually made from white Riesling, Sylvaner, or Müller-Thurgau grapes.

SACCHAROMETER: A hydrometer scaled to indicate sugar contained in a solution. See Hydrometer.

SAUTERNES: Wines made in the Bordeaux region of France from mainly Sauvignon and Semillon grapes that have been desiccated by the action of the *Botrytis cinerea* mold to extreme sweetness. A dessert wine par excellence.

SHERRY: Wine made from grapes with much sugar. Secondary fermentation in the presence of air and special *flor* yeast develops distinctive flavor. A fortified wine.

SIPHON: To transfer liquid from one container to a lower container by means of a tube, utilizing gravity flow.

STILL WINE: Wine that contains no entrapped carbon dioxide to create bubbles, or effervescence.

STUCK FERMENTATION: Fermentation that started, then stopped usually because of drastic change in temperature.

SULFURING: Addition of sulfur dioxide to wine or must to kill undesirable microorganisms and prevent oxidation of the wine.

SWEET WINE: Wine that contains approximately 3 per cent or more of unfermented sugar.

TANNIC ACID, TANNIN: Astringent material found in oak cooperage, grape seeds and stems, and in other fruit. A desirable addition to wine in small quantities, preserving and flavoring wine.

TABLE WINES: Dry wines containing approximately 12 per cent alcohol. Used in cooking and consumption of foods.

VAT: A large open container used for fermentation and similar cellar operations.

VINOSITY: A flavor associated with wines that develops during the maturing process.

VINTAGE: The yearly harvest of grapes. Wines made from grapes picked in a certain year are usually identified as belonging to that year.

VITIS VINIFERA: European wine-grape varieties, extensively planted throughout the world.

WATER SEAL: A small container of water in which a tube terminates. The tube allows carbon dioxide generated during fermentation to escape, while the water prevents air from entering the closed fermentation vessel.

YEAST STARTER: A preliminary fermentation using a sterile sugar solution; allows increase of small amounts of yeast to large enough colonies to initiate rapid, active fermentation of large amounts of must.

Bibliography

Allen, H. Warner. *The Romance of Wine*. New York: Dutton, 1932.

Amerine, M. A., Berg, H. W., and Cruess, W. V. *The Technology of Wine Making*. Westport, Conn.: Avi Publishing Co., Inc., 1967. 2nd ed.

Amerine, M. A., and Joslyn, M. A. *Table Wines: The Technology of Their Production*. Berkeley and Los Angeles: Univ. of Calif. Press, 1970.

Amerine, M. A., and Ough, C. S. *Effects of Temperature on Wine Making*. Calif. Agri. Exper. Sta. Bulletin 827, 1966.

Amerine, M. A., and Singleton, V. L. *Wine, An Introduction for Americans*. Berkeley and Los Angeles: Univ. of Calif. Press, 1968.

Amerine, M. A., and Winkler, A. J. *California Wine Grapes: Composition and Quality of Their Musts and Wines*. Calif. Agri. Exper. Sta. Bulletin 794, 1963.

Anon. *Mrs. Beeton's Family Cookery*. London: Ward, Locke & Co., 1915.

Anon. *The Housekeeper's Receipt Book, or The Repository of Domestic Knowledge*. London: S. A. Oddy, 1813.

Anon. *The Family Receipt Book*. Pittsburgh: Barnes, 1819.

Anon. *The Cook's Own Book, being a complete culinary encyclopedia*. Boston, Munroe & Francis, 1832.

Anon. *Enquire Within upon Everything*. London: Houlston & Sons, 1899. 95th ed.

Anon. *The Farm and Household Cyclopaedia, A Complete and Ready Reference*. New York: F. M. Lupton, 1888.

Anon. *The Successful House-Keeper*. Detroit: M. S. Ellsworth, 1883.

Cato, Marcus Porcius (The Elder). *De Agri Cultura*. London: W. Heinemann, 1954.

Chapman, F. M., and Chapman, Chas. C. *The American Encyclopedia of Practical Knowledge*. Topeka, Kan.: Montgomery & Williams, 1888.

Chase, A. W., M.D. *Dr. Chase's Recipes; or, Information for Everybody*. Ann Arbor, Mich.: privately printed, 1867. 47th ed.

Child, Lydia M. *The American Frugal House Wife*. Boston: Carter, 1838. 16th ed.

Clark, J. Harold. *Small Fruits for Your Home Garden*. Garden City, N.Y.: Doubleday, 1958.

Columella, Lucius Junius Moderatus (tr. E. S. Forster, E. H. Heffner). *Res Rustica* (On Agriculture). Cambridge, Mass.: Harvard Univ. Press, 1941.

Croly, Mrs. J. C. *Jennie June's American Cookery Book*. New York: Excelsior, 1878.

Dorozynski, Alexander, and Bell, Bibiane. *The Wine Book*. New York.: The Golden Press, 1969.

Escoffier, A. *Guide Culinaire*. London: W. Heinemann, 1907.

Farley, John. *The London Art of Cookery, and Housekeeper's Complete Assistant*. London: J. Scatsherd & J. Whitaker & G. & T. Wilkie, 1792. 7th ed.

Fessler, Julius. *Guideline to Practical Winemaking*. Oakland, Calif.: Fessler, 1968.

Fox, Helen M. *Gardening with Herbs*. New York: Macmillan, 1940.

Francatelli, C. E. *Francatelli's Modern Cook*. Philadelphia: David McKay, n.d., 26th ed.

Haraszthy, Agostin. *Grape Culture, Wines and Winemaking, with Notes upon Agriculture and Horticulture*. New York: Harper & Bros., 1862.

Hardwick, Homer. *Winemaking at Home*. New York: W. Funk, 1954.

Hendrick, U. P. *Grapes and Wines from Home Vineyards*. New York: Oxford Univ. Press, 1945.

Hiss, Emil. *The Standard Manual of Soda and Other Beverages*. Chicago: Englehard, 1897.

Hopkins, Albert A. (ed.). *The Scientific American Cyclopedia of Receipts, Notes and Queries*. New York: Munn & Co., 1909. 27th ed.

Hussmann, George C. *American Grape Growing and Wine Making*. New York: Orange Judd Co., 1833.

Hyams, Edward. *Dionysus, A Social History of Wine*. London: Thames and Hudson, 1965.

Kitchener, Wm., M.D. *The Cook's Oracle*. Edinburgh: Cadell, 1843.

Lucia, Salvatore P., M.D. *Wine as Food and Medicine*. New York: Blakiston, 1954.

Mackenzie. *Five Thousand Receipts in All the Useful and Domestic Arts.* Philadelphia: James Kay & Brother, 1829.

Markham, Gervase. *The English Housewife.* London: H. Sawbridge, 1683. 9th ed.

Moxon, Elizabeth. *English Housewifery.* Leeds: G. Wright, 1764.

National Feder. Women's Institutes. *Homemade Wines Syrups & Cordials.* London: F. W. Beech, 1954.

Ough, C. S., and Amerine, M. A. "Studies with Controlled Fermentation Effects of Temperature on Rates, Composition and Quality of Wines," *American Journal Enology & Viticult.* ⋕ 12, 1961.

Pepys, Samuel. *Diary.* New York: C. T. Brainerd, 188?

Phin, John. *Open Air Grape Culture, a Practical Treatise on Garden and Vineyard Culture of the Vine, and the Manufacture of Domestic Wine.* New York: C. M. Saxton, 1863.

Plat, Sir Hugh. *Delights for Ladies* (1609). London: C. Lockwood, 1948.

Prato, Katherina. *Süddeutsche Küche.* Graz and Wien: Verlagsbuchhandlung Styria, 1922. 71st ed.

Rack, John. *The French Wine and Liquor Manufacturer.* New York: Fitzgerald, n.d., 4th ed.

Raffald, Elizabeth. *The Experienced English Housekeeper.* London: R. Baldwin, 1769.

Rundell, Mrs. Maria E. *A New System of Domestic Cookery, Formed upon Principles of Economy,* by A Lady. London: J. Murray, 1808.

Seltman, Charles. *Wine in the Ancient World.* London: Routledge & Kegan Paul Ltd., 1957.

Simon, André. *The Wines, Vineyards and Vignerons of Australia.* London: Paul Hamlyn, 1967.

Smith, E. *The Compleat Housewife; or Accomplished Gentlewoman's Companion.* London: privately printed, 1753.

Smith, Mary Stuart. *The Virginia Cookery Book.* New York: Harper, 1885.

Tilton, Mrs. E. S. *Home Dissertations—An Offering to the Household.* San Francisco: Goldberg, Bowen & Co., 1891.

U. S. Internal Revenue Service. "Wine," Part 240 of Title 26, Code of Federal Regulations. Washington, D.C.: U. S. Government Printing Office, July 1970.

Varro, Marcus Terentius. *Rerum Rusticarum* (tr. Wm. Davis Hooper, Rev. H. B. Ash). Cambridge, Mass.: Harvard Univ. Press, 1944.

Verral, William. *The Cook's Paradise, A Complete System of Cookery* (1759). London: Sylvan Press, 1948.

Vidal, J.-L. *La Viticulture.* Paris: Delarue, n.d.

Wagner, Philip. A *Wine Grower's Guide.* New York: Alfred A. Knopf, 1945.

Wagner, Philip. *American Wines and How to Make Them.* New York: Alfred A. Knopf, 1933.

Waugh, A. *In Praise of Wine and Certain Noble Spirits.* New York: Wm. Sloan Assoc., 1959.

Wickson, Edw. J. *California Fruits and How to Grow Them.* San Francisco: Rural Press, 1921. 9th ed.

Wright, Helen S. *Old-Time Recipes for Home Made Wines Cordials and Liqueurs.* Boston: Page, 1909.

Younger, William. *Gods, Men and Wine.* Cleveland: World, 1966.

Appendix

LATIN NAMES OF HERBS USED IN WINE MAKING

ALEXANDER . . . . *Smyrnium olusatrum*

BALM . . . . *Melissa officinalis*

BARBERRY . . . . Berries of *Berberis vulgaris*

BENJAMIN . . . . *Styrax benzoin*

BETONY . . . . *Stachys betonica*

BLESSED THISTLE . . . . *Carbenia benedicta*

BORAGE . . . . *Borago officinalis*

BURNET . . . . *Sanguisorba officinalis*

CALAMUS . . . . *Acorus calamus*

CARDAMOM . . . . *Elettaria cardamomum*

CELANDINE . . . . *Chelidonium majus*

CENTAURY . . . . *Erythraea centaurium*

CLARY . . . . *Salvia sclarea*

CLOVE GILLIFLOWER . . . . *Dianthus caryophyllus*

COMFREY . . . . *Symphytum officinale*

EGLANTINE . . . . *Rosa eglanteria*

FENUGREEK . . . . *Trigonella foenum-graecum*

GOLDENROD . . . . *Solidago virgaurea*

GRAINS OF PARADISE . . . . *Amomum melegueta*

HEARTSEASE . . . . *Viola tricolor*

HOREHOUND . . . . *Marrubium vulgare*

JUJUBES . . . . fruit of *Zizyphus*

LIVERWORT . . . . *Anemone hepatica*

LOVAGE . . . . *Levisticum officinale*

MALLOW . . . . *Malva sylvestris*

MARSH MALLOW . . . . *Althaea officinalis*

MOTHERWORT . . . . *Leonurus cardiaca*

MUGWORT . . . . *Artemisia vulgaris*

MULLEIN or MULLEN . . . . *Verbascum thapsus*

ORRICE . . . . Orris, Root of *Iris florentina*

ORIGANY . . . . *Origanum*

PELLITORY OF THE WALL . . . . *Parietaria officinalis*

PENNYROYAL . . . . *Mentha pulegium*

PIMPERNEL . . . . *Anagallis arvensis*

ROMAN WORMWOOD . . . . *Artemisia pontica*

RUE . . . . *Ruta graveolens*

SAGE . . . . *Salvia officinalis*

ST.-JOHN'S-WORT . . . . *Hypericum perforatum*

SALOP . . . . Dried *Orchis* tubers

SASSAFRAS . . . . *Sassafras officinalis*

SAVORY . . . . *Satureia hortensis*

SAXIFRAGE . . . . *Pimpinella saxifraga*

SCURVY GRASS . . . . *Cochlearia officinalis*

SHEPHERD'S-PURSE . . . . *Capsella bursa-pastoris*

SOUTHERNWOOD . . . . *Artemisia abrotanum*

SPEARMINT . . . . *Mentha viridis*

SPIKENARD . . . . *Aralia racemosa*

SUCCORY or CHICORY . . . . *Cichorium intybus*

SWEETBRIER . . . . *Rosa eglanteria*

TANSY . . . . *Tanacetum vulgare*

VERONICA . . . . *Veronica officinalis*

VIRGINIA SNAKEROOT . . . . *Aristolochia serpentaria*

WATER BETONY . . . . *Scrophularia aquatica*

WOODBINE . . . . *Gelsemium nitidum*

WORMWOOD . . . . *Artemisia absinthium*

YARROW . . . . *Achillea millefolium*

CONVERSION TABLES

VOLUME

1 cubic centimeter	= 0.061 cubic inch
1 cubic inch	= 16.387 cubic centimeters
1 cubic meter	= 35.314 cubic feet
1 cubic foot	= 0.028 cubic meter
1 cubic meter	= 1.308 cubic yards
1 cubic yard	= 0.7646 cubic meter

MASS

1 gram	= 15.432 grains
1 grain	= 0.065 gram
1 gram	= 0.035 ounce avoirdupois
1 ounce avoirdupois	= 28.3495 grams
1 gram	= 0.032 ounce troy
1 ounce troy	= 31.1035 grams
1 pound avoirdupois	= 0.4536 kilogram
1 kilogram	= 2.2046 pounds

CAPACITY

1 milliliter	= 0.034 ounce U.S. liquid
1 ounce U.S. liquid	= 29.573 milliliters
1 dram (U.S. apothecaries')	= 3.6966 milliliters
1 liter	= 1.057 quarts U.S. liquid
1 quart U.S. liquid	= 0.946 liter
1 gallon	= 3.785 liters
⅕ gallon U.S.	= 25.6 ounces, or 75.707 centiliters

WEIGHTS AND MEASURES

1 ton	= 20 hundredweight
	= 80 quarters = 2,240 pounds
16 drachms	= 1 ounce
16 ounces	= 1 pound
28 pounds	= 1 quarter
4 quarters	= 1 hundredweight (112 pounds)
20 hundredweight	= 1 ton (2,240 pounds)
27.344 grains	= 1 drachm
16 drachms	= 1 ounce
1 stone	= 14 pounds
1 quintal	= 100 pounds
1 teaspoon	= 1⅓ fluid drachms = 80 drops
	= 36.457 grains
1 dessertspoon	= 2½ fluid drachms
1 tablespoon	= 4 fluid drachms, or ½ ounce
1 wineglass	= 4–6 fluid ounces
1 teacupful	= 6 fluid ounces
1 tumblerful	= 10 fluid ounces
1 thimbleful	= ¾ fluid drachm
pinch (leaves, flowers)	= 1 drachm (troy)
handful ″ ″	= 10 drachms (troy)

LIQUID MEASURE

Dash	= 6 drops (0.075 teaspoon)
Teaspoon	= ⅙ ounce
Tablespoon	= ½ ounce
Pony	= 1 ounce
Jigger	= 1½ ounces
Large jigger	= 2 ounces
Split	= 6½ to 8 ounces
Half pint	= 8 ounces
Tenth	= 12.8 ounces
Half bottle (champagne)	= 13 ounces
Pint	= 16 ounces
Bottle (wine)	= 24 ounces (European) 25.6 ounces (United States)
Bottle (champagne)	= 26 ounces
Fifth	= 25.6 ounces
Bottle (vermouth)	= 30 ounces
Quart	= 32 ounces
Liter	= 33.8 ounces
Imperial quart	= 38.4 ounces
Magnum (2 bottles)	= 52 ounces
Double magnum jeroboam	= 104 ounces
Gallon	= 128 ounces
Rehoboam	= 156 ounces (1.22 gallons)
Methuselah	= 208 ounces (1.63 gallons)
Salmanasar	= 312 ounces (2.44 gallons)
Balthazar	= 416 ounces (3.3 gallons)
Nebuchadnezzar	= 520 ounces (4.07 gallons)
Demijohn	= 627.2 ounces (4.9 gallons)

In exploration of old books, the following measurements may sometimes be found. Present-day equivalents are given.

DRY MEASURE

2 gallons	= 1 peck
4 pecks or 8 gallons	= 1 bushel
2 bushels	= 1 strike
4 bushels	= 1 coomb
5 bushels	= 1 sack
8 bushels	= 1 quarter

OLD WINE MEASURES

4 gills, or quaterns	= 1 pint		
2 pints	= 1 quart		
4 quarts	= 1 gallon	= .833	imperial gallon
10 gallons	= 1 anchor	= 8.33	″ gallons
18 gallons	= 1 bunlet	= 15	″ ″
31½ gallons	= 1 barrel	= 26.25	″ ″
42 gallons	= 1 tierce	= 35	″ ″
63 gallons, or 2 barrels	= 1 hogshead	= 52.5	″ ″
84 gallons, or 1⅓ hogsheads	= 1 puncheon	= 70	″ ″
126 gallons, or 2 hogsheads	= 1 pipe, or butt	= 105	″ ″
2 pipes or 3 puncheons	= 1 tun		

U.S. MEASURE

4 gills	= 1 pint
2 pints	= 1 quart
4 quarts	= 1 gallon
63 gallons	= 1 hogshead
2 hogsheads	= 1 pipe, or butt
2 pipes	= 1 tun

TABLE FOR ADDITION OF SUGAR TO RAISE
1 GALLON OF JUICE TO 25° BALLING

DEGREES BALLING OF JUICE	POUNDS OF CANE OR BEET SUGAR
0	2.77
1	2.67
2	2.57
3	2.47
4	2.37
5	2.26
6	2.16
7	2.05
8	1.95
9	1.84
10	1.73
11	1.62
12	1.51
13	1.40
14	1.29
15	1.18
16	1.06
17	.95
18	.83
19	.72
20	.60
21	.48
22	.36
23	.24
24	.12

TABLE FOR REDUCTION OF CONCENTRATES
TO REDUCE THE BALLING OF CONCENTRATES
TO NOMINAL 24°

DEGREES BALLING OF CONCENTRATE	GALLONS OF WATER PER GALLON OF CONCENTRATE
40	0.7851
41	0.8378
42	0.8910
43	0.9447
44	0.9988
45	1.0533
46	1.1084
47	1.1639
48	1.2199
49	1.2764
50	1.3334
51	1.3909
52	1.4490
53	1.5075
54	1.5665
55	1.6260
56	1.6861
57	1.7467
58	1.8078
59	1.8695
60	1.9317

On the average, 5.8 ounces of water should be added to each gallon of concentrate to reduce the concentration 1 degree Balling.

TABLE FOR ADDITION OF TARTARIC ACID

IF ACID PRESENT IS GRAMS PER LITER	ADD PER GALLON FOR 0.6 PER CENT	ADD PER GALLON FOR 0.7 PER CENT
3	11.4 grams	15.2 grams
3.5	9.5 "	13.3 "
4	7.6 "	11.4 "
4.5	5.7 "	9.5 "
5	3.8 "	7.6 "
5.5	1.9 "	5.7 "
6	0.0 "	3.8 "
6.5	0.0 "	1.9 "

TABLE FOR ADDITION OF SINGLE-STRENGTH PECTOLYTIC ENYZME

FERMENTATION TEMPERATURE TO BE USED	ADD PER GALLON WHITE WINE OR FRUIT WINE	ADD PER GALLON RED WINE
50° F	0.45 gram	
55° F	0.40 "	0.59 gram
60° F	0.35 "	0.45 "
65° F	0.30 "	0.40 "
70° F		0.35 "

SOLUTION FORMULAS

Iodine N/40 Solution

Dissolve 3.2 grams chemically pure iodine crystals and 6.3 grams chemically pure potassium iodide into enough distilled water to total one liter. Mix well, and keep in refrigerator when not being used.

1% Starch Solution

Weigh out 1 gram soluble powdered starch, add it to 25 milliliters distilled water, and stir well. Heat the solution until it becomes clear. Cool the liquid and add enough denatured alcohol to bring the amount of liquid back to exactly 25 milliliters.

25% Sulfuric Acid

Buy sulfuric acid at larger hardware stores.
Measure 77 milliliters distilled water into a 200-ml Pyrex beaker. Set the beaker containing the water in a sink that is partly filled with cool water. Add 23 milliliters of concentrated sulfuric acid slowly to the water, stirring with a glass rod. Allow it to remain a half hour before pouring into the storage vessel.

1% Phenolphthalein Solution (1% $C_{20}H_{14}O_4$)

Weigh out ¼ gram powdered phenolphthalein, and add enough denatured alcohol (ethanol) to make 25 milliliters.

One-Tenth Normal Sodium Hydroxide Solution (NaOH N/10)

Weigh out 4 grams chemically pure sodium hydroxide fragments, and drop these into enough water to make one liter. To check this against a one-tenth normal hydrochloric acid solution, withdraw 20 milliliters one-tenth normal sodium hydroxide solution into a clean flask. Add 3 to 6 drops of 1% phenolphthalein solution. Fill a clean burette with one-tenth normal hydrochloric acid solution, and titrate into the sodium hydroxide solution until the pink color disappears. A properly balanced solution should require exactly 20 milliliters of one-tenth normal hydrochloric acid to remove pink color. If more than 20 milliliters of hydrochloric acid is required, the sodium hydroxide solution is too strong and should be diluted with additional distilled water. If less hydrochloric acid is needed, more solid sodium hydroxide should be added until the solution balances with the acid when titrated.

TEST FOR FREE SULFUR DIOXIDE IN WINE

Place 20 milliliters of the wine to be tested in a flask, using a pipette for accurate measurement. Add 3 to 4 drops 25% sulfuric acid and several drops of 1% starch solution. Fill a 25-ml burette with 40/N iodine solution and drip it into the flask. When the liquid turns blue-black, stop and note the number of milliliters of the iodine solution that have been used. Each 0.1 milliliter of iodine used is equivalent to four parts per million of sulfur dioxide in the wine. For example: if 1.7 milliliters of iodine solution was used, 1.0 ml=40 ppm, 0.7 ml=28 ppm, therefore 1.7 ml=68 ppm.

LIST OF SUPPLIERS OF WINE MAKING EQUIPMENT AND MATERIALS

This list is by no means complete, but represents dealers in several parts of the country who supply wine making ingredients and materials. They are all active as of the date of writing.

AETNA BOTTLE COMPANY
708 Rainier Avenue South, Seattle, Wash. 98144

BACCHANALIA
Box 312-Z-7
Saugatuck Station, Westport, Conn. 06880

BEARARDUCCI BROS. MFG. CO.
McKeesport, Pa. 15132

COMPLEAT WINEMAKER
P. O. Box 2470
Yountville, Calif. 94599

NICHOLS GARDEN NURSERY
1190 North Pacific Highway
Albany, Ore. 97321

PRESQUE ISLE WINE CELLARS
9440 Buffalo Road
North East, Pa. 16428

SEMPLEX OF USA
Box 12276
Minneapolis, Minn. 55412

WERTH WINE
P. O. Box 1902
Cedar Rapids, Iowa 52406

WINE-ART, INC.
4324 Geary Boulevard
San Francisco, Calif. 94118

WINE-ART SANTA BARBARA
3532 State Street
Santa Barbara, Calif. 93105

THE WYNE TABLE
P. O. Box 490
Norman, Okla. 73069

A. R. ZACHER CO., INC.
P. O. Box 1006
Fresno, Calif. 93714

REGIONAL OFFICES OF THE INTERNAL REVENUE SERVICE ALCOHOL, TOBACCO, AND FIREARMS DIVISION

CENTRAL REGION
Indiana, Kentucky, Michigan, Ohio, West Virginia

550 Main Street
Cincinnati, Ohio 45202

MID-ATLANTIC REGION
Delaware, Maryland, New Jersey, Pennsylvania, Virginia, District of Columbia

2 Penn Center Plaza
Philadelphia, Pa. 19102

MIDWEST
Illinois, Iowa, Minnesota, Missouri, North Dakota, South Dakota, Wisconsin

35 E. Wacker Drive
Chicago, Ill. 60601

NORTH ATLANTIC
Connecticut, Maine, Massachusetts, New Hampshire, New York, Rhode Island, Vermont

90 Church Street
New York, N.Y. 10007

SOUTHEAST
Alabama, Florida, Georgia, Mississippi, North Carolina, South Carolina, Tennessee

275 Peachtree Street N.E.
Atlanta, Ga. 30303

SOUTHWEST
Arkansas, Colorado, Kansas, Louisiana, New Mexico, Oklahoma, Texas, Wyoming

1114 Commerce Street
Dallas, Tex. 75202

WESTERN
Alaska, Arizona, California, Hawaii, Idaho, Montana, Nevada, Oregon, Utah, Washington.

870 Market Street
San Francisco, Calif. 94102

CONVERSION TABLE FOR PARTS PER MILLION

The amount of sulfur dioxide in musts and wine is frequently expressed in parts per million (ppm). The following table shows the amount of *fresh* potassium metabisulfite to be added to wines and musts to provide the following ppm of sulfur dioxide. The table is based upon the generally accepted figure of 50% sulfur dioxide being released from potassium metabisulfite in solution.

TO OBTAIN SO$_2$ CONCENTRATION OF:

ppm *add grams potassium metabisulfite per*	1 GALLON	5 GALLONS
10	.075	.38
20	.15	.75
30	.226	1.13
40	.3	1.5
50	.38	1.87
60	.45	2.2
70	.53	2.6
80	.6	3.0
90	.68	3.38
100	.75	3.78

GENERAL:

1 ppm = 0.058416 grain per gallon
1 ppm = 0.001 gram per liter
1 ppm = 0.00378 gram per liter
1 part potassium metabisulfite = ½ part sulfur dioxide

COMMON NAMES OF SOME CHEMICALS USED IN WINE MAKING, TESTING, EQUIPMENT CLEANING, ETC.

Sodium carbonate; sal soda; washing soda; salt of soda; natron; soda ash	$Na_2CO_310H_2O$
Sodium hydroxide; caustic soda	$NaOH$
Potassium borotrate; soluble cream of tartar	$K_4B_4O_8$
Potassium carbonate; pearlash; potash; salt of tartar	K_2CO_3
Potassium hydroxide; potassium hydrate; caustic potash	KOH
Potassium tartrate; soluble tartrate; neutral tartrate of potassium	$K_2C_4H_4O_6$
Potassium bitartrate; Argol; cream of tartar; crystals of tartar	$KHC_4H_4O_6$
Calcium carbonate; chalk; limestone; marble; calcite	$CaCO_3$
Calcium sulphate; gypsum; plaster of Paris	$CaSO_4 \cdot 2H_2O$
Malic acid	$H_2 \cdot C_4H_4O_5$
Lactic acid	$H \cdot C_3H_5O_3$
Bentonite; Wyoming clay	
Tartaric acid	$H_2 \cdot C_4H_4O_6$
Citric acid	$H_3 \cdot C_6H_5O_7$

Index

Figures in italics refer to illustrations.

/